THE 30-DAY NOVEL AND BEYOND!

A TRAINING PROGRAM FOR ASPIRING NOVELISTS

STEFON MEARS

Thousand
Faces
Publishing

Also by Stefon Mears

Cavan Oltblood Series
Half a Wizard
The Ice Dagger
Spells of Undeath

Spells for Hire
Devil's Shoestring
Zombie Powder
Spirit Trap
Dragon's Blood

The Rise of Magic
Magician's Choice
Sleight of Mind
Lunar Alchemy
Three Fae Monte
The Sphinx Principle
Double Backed Magic

The Telepath Trilogy
Surviving Telepathy
Immoral Telepathy
Targeting Telepathy

Edge of Humanity
Caught Between Monsters
Hunting Monsters

Power City Tales
Not Quite Bulletproof
No Money in Heroism

Sects and the City
Prince of a Thousand Worlds (coming soon)
Longhairs and Short Tales: A Collection of Cat Stories
Devil's Night
Portal-Land, Oregon
Stealing from Pirates
Fade to Gold
With a Broken Sword
Twice Against the Dragon
The House on Cedar Street
Sudden Death
On the Edge of Faerie
Confronting Legends (Spells & Swords Vol. 1)
Uncle Stone Teeth and Other Macabre Poems
The Patreon Collection, Vol. 1-5 (Vol. 6, coming soon)
The 30-Day Novel and Beyond!

Published by Thousand Faces Publishing, Portland, Oregon

http://1kfaces.com

Copyright © 2020 by Stefon Mears

Front cover image © Ryan Deberardinis | Dreamstime.com (File ID: 29082295)

Front cover image © Dmitrii Kiselev | Dreamstime.com (File ID: 24331537)

ISBN: 978-1-948490-22-1

The
30-Day Novel
and
Beyond!

A training program for aspiring novelists

CONTENTS

CHAPTER THREE

CHAPTER FOUR

CHAPTER FIVE

CHAPTER SIX

INTRODUCTION

I've wanted to be a writer most of my life.

Heck, I remember graduating from college back in 1992 and talking to my father one night about my wanting to write professionally.

He liked the idea. Fully supportive. I could've gone for it.

I almost did.

But then I read an interview with Harlan Ellison. I don't remember where I read it, or what his exact words were, I'm afraid. But I'll always remember the essence of one thing he said.

He warned, basically, that writing was a hell of a way to make a living. That no one should do it unless they couldn't do anything else.

Now, for context, I grew up in a house full of books. Including many written or edited by Ellison. I couldn't tell you how many times the man and his stories came up in family conversations over the years.

So when I read that interview, I took the implicit advice from a man I'd never met.

I tried to do anything else.

For more than *ten years*, I tried to do anything else. I must've tried my hand at more than a dozen different office jobs. But each time I somehow ended up writing and editing.

I edited reseller contracts for Hewlett Packard. I clarified English translations of Japanese video games. I wrote procedural and technical documents for companies so small they probably don't exist anymore. Advertising copy. Fundraising letters. Grant applications for a private school. And more. So much more.

Didn't matter where I worked or what my job title (or official duties) were. I ended up writing and editing.

Yet somehow, that wasn't enough to give me the clue I needed.

No.

My moment of revelation came one evening while I sat reading on my bed. I had the album *Soul Cadillac* by the Cherry Poppin' Daddies playing in the background.

The song "Irish Whiskey" came on. It's about a man who abandoned his dreams for the sake of making money for his family. Now he's old. He hates his life. He resents his family. And all he has is Irish whiskey.

Cold fear jolted the book out of my hands. Washed over my skin. Prickled the back of my neck.

A moment of true mortal terror that one day I would become that man.

I started writing again that night.

Only problem. I had no real idea what I was doing.

I agonized over every word. Every sentence. And I often went back and re-wrote whole passages because I thought I might be using "to be" verbs too often.

I struggled. I did everything wrong. But I kept at it.

Took me six months to write a short story.

It got rejected, of course, from the first place I sent it. Not because the story was bad, either, though I didn't understand that at the time.

No. It got rejected unread because I hadn't followed standard manuscript format. Didn't even know what it was.

I had the will. I had the ideas. But I lacked the skills. And I wasn't sure how to go about getting them.

I twiddled about that way with writing for a couple of years. Occasionally flinging words onto the page with wild abandon, then spending weeks agonizing over a scant few pages.

I did a lot more thinking than writing. And finishing anything at all was a major effort.

My biggest accomplishments during that period were a handful of credits in the world of roleplaying games. I might have tried to go that direction full time, but bad experiences had soured me on the industry.

Finally, I reached a point where I had to admit I was getting nowhere. I needed to either commit — find and take some classes, learn what I was doing, and really go for it — or I needed to quit pretending and do something else.

I realized then, I didn't really trust that I could do it. That I could write even one novel, let alone several.

I dithered about in my writing because that was the safe thing to do. I could call myself a writer, without the risk of finishing something and *giving it to people to read*.

Maybe even having the audacity to *charge* something for my efforts. What a concept.

I needed a litmus test. Some way to either prove to myself that I could really write, or demonstrate that I should give up and do something else.

Enter National Novel Writing Month, often just called NaNoWriMo. A challenge to write a fifty-thousand-word novel in thirty days, during the month of November.

It sounded terrifying.

It also sounded like something that a professional writer should be able to do.

Yes. I decided to take their thirty-day novel challenge, and let the results prove whether or not I could make it as a writer.

On November 1st, 2007, somewhere around eight o'clock in the evening, I sat down and started writing my first novel. Twenty-two days and about fifty-four thousand words later, I finished it. *Telepathy*

1A, the struggles of a college freshman who spontaneously develops the power to read minds.

As of this writing, I've published more than twenty novels, another dozen or so novellas, and more than a hundred and thirty short stories.

And I have more coming all the time.

But here's the thing.

Every November, a great many people across the world take a similar challenge and try to write a novel in thirty days. The vast majority of them don't go on to start careers in writing.

For some of them, that might be by choice. But for others, it might be that they're doing it wrong.

Well. What *I* would consider doing it wrong. But I don't think in terms of crossing a single goal line and stopping. I think in terms of telling stories and developing a career.

That's why I'm writing this book. To talk about how to use a thirty-day novel challenge the way I did.

To use it as a test about whether or not you, too, could have a career as a writer. And maybe to help you get started on that career.

I've got my fingers crossed for you.

CHAPTER ONE

SOME BASICS

IS THIS BOOK FOR YOU?

THAT'S REALLY THE QUESTION, ISN'T IT? I THINK THAT'S WHAT WE ALL wonder, as we peruse books in bookstores or online. There are already so many books about writing, how can you know whether or not this is a book that will help you?

Well, the way I look at it, there are about four categories of writers who might benefit from this book.

1. The Aspiring Writers

Maybe you have an idea for a novel or series. Maybe you've written a little. Maybe you've got a handful of finished stories on your hard drive, but you've never made the jump from flash fiction or short stories to novels, and want to know if you're capable of more.

This is where I was, back in 2007. Heck, I had some published works to my credit, but I still questioned whether or not I could write one novel, let alone several.

If this is you, then I think this book should help you figure out where you are as a writer. And just maybe, help you surprise yourself in the best way possible.

2. The Hobbyists

There are those who say that if you love what you do, you'll never work a day in your life. On the other hand are those who say that if you make your hobby your job, you'll learn to hate what you love.

I think most hobbyists are caught between those ideas. Wondering if they could get paid to play with stories for the rest of their lives, or if adding the pressure to produce would turn what they love into what they hate.

If this is you, I think this book will help you figure out your answer. Because when you write as a hobby, you can do it when you feel like it, and do other things when you don't.

And you don't even have to *show* your writing to anyone if you don't feel like it.

Well, if you stick with me, you'll have to hit a deadline. And then we'll talk about what to do with your finished novel. Because I don't want it just sitting on your hard drive, collecting e-dust.

3. Short Story Writers Looking to Stretch

There are those who can and do write short stories. Even submit them to magazines and anthologies and sell them from time to time. But the thought of writing something longer stresses them out.

If this is you, I think this book should help you work your way up to longer stories. You're already an experienced storyteller. You just need a way to stretch up to something longer. I think the exercises in this book can help with that.

4. The Experienced Novelists?

There are those who already write novels. What good could this book do them?

Well, if this is you, whether or not this could help you may depend on two things.

If you have trouble letting yourself come up with ideas, my writing exercise regimen may help you.

If you only write with an outline, I can help you let go of those outlines and learn to write into the dark. Maybe that's not for you, but maybe it is. Never know until you've tried it...

5. Other?

So even if you're an experienced writer, good with your ideas, and you already write into the dark, should you still bother with this book?

One thing I've learned over the years. You never know when something is going to strike you just right. I may say something that triggers a revelation for you.

I say it's worth a shot. But it's your money.

TO NANO OR NOT TO NANO

When I did my thirty-day novel challenge, I did it by participating in National Novel Writing Month.

Does that mean you should too?

Honestly, it doesn't matter. You can set the start and end dates of your own thirty-day novel challenge whenever you want.

So, if November is a bad month for you, in terms of trying this, well, then just pick one of the other eleven months and go to it.

Well.

All right.

Technically, if you pick February, you're either shorting yourself a day or two, or you're bleeding into January or March.

But hey! It's your challenge. If you want to start on Tax Day (April April 15th here in the U.S.) or your birthday, or Talk Like a Pirate Day, go for it! As long as you give yourself a thirty-day deadline, to stay true to the challenge.

That doesn't really answer the question though.

Should you try the challenge as part of NaNoWriMo or not?

It depends on what kind of person you are. I don't mean that in a judgmental kind of way. I mean it in the sense of figuring out how *you* work best.

For me, I'm private about this kind of thing. I don't write in groups. If I write in a public place, I tend to tuck myself away and ignore the world. I don't want anyone to interrupt me, or ask what I'm writing, and so on.

I don't talk about challenges, either, until they're done. I just do them or I don't.

And yet, I did my challenge as part of NaNoWriMo all the same. And I did it for the same reason I might run a 10K someday, instead of just trying to run ten kilometers on my treadmill.

The power of it being an official challenge meant something to me. A challenge where someone else set my start and end dates. Gave me my deadlines. It reminded me of being in school, and I was a very good student.

So that was a motivator for me. It helped, to know it wasn't just me deciding to do it. I had an outside force to answer to.

Heck, I still take challenges from the outside world sometimes. Earlier this year I completed a challenge to write a new short story every week for a year. And those challenges have power for me.

So if the thought of having *someone else* set the rules helps you, then I say do your challenge as part of NaNoWriMo.

Along similar lines, some people benefit from camaraderie. I have friends — professional writers — who like to get together once a month in one of their living rooms and write together. They don't talk, except at specified break times or when they're done for the day. They just sit with their laptops and write. And that works for them.

NaNoWriMo can give you that. They have local organizers who plan write-ins and the like. Or they did the last time I looked at their website.

So if that sort of thing appeals to you, gives you a little lift inside, then, again, participating in NaNoWriMo might be for you.

I can only really advise you so far about this part. I'd suggest you check out their website (nanowrimo.org), look around, and see what you think.

Trust your gut here. If it feels appealing, go for it. If it doesn't, forget it, and try the challenge on your own.

A WARNING

I know a lot of writers these days.

Most of them got their starts without any thirty-day novel challenge at all. (Though some of those individuals attempt one annually anyway.)

Writing fiction — telling stories — is a strange thing to do.

Look at it this way. I happily spend hours and hours alone in my office, five days a week, making up lies about people who don't exist.

And I get emotionally invested in those made-up people. I care deeply about them, even while putting them through horrible struggles.

And even more than that aspect, the methods of writing fiction are idiosyncratic as hell. I don't think any two novelists really do things the same way.

For example, I know that science fiction and fantasy author Kevin J. Anderson often writes by dictating into a recorder while hiking.

I've tried that a few times. Drives me nuts. I like having the keyboard under my fingertips, and letting the thoughts flow through that way.

Some writers I know need silence to write. Others must have music, or white noise, or whatever. Some have trained themselves to write standing up, while others insist on sitting in their favorite chairs.

I even know a writer who likes to bang a gong every time he sits down to write. (Or used to. I don't know if he still does that.)

Why is this a warning?

Because while all fiction writers tell stories, we do so in very different ways. We *think* story in very different ways.

It's important to recognize this.

My approach to the thirty-day novel challenge worked for *me*. I'm going to show you how I did it, in case it works for you too.

But it might not. And that's all right.

At the end of the day, the only one who knows whether or not you can write novels is you. Not me. Not your parents. Not your teachers. Not your friends and lovers.

Only you really know.

Well, and possibly your pets. It's amazing how much your pets know about you.

I'm pretty sure that my cats were trying to tell me for years that I should be writing. It's on me that I didn't listen.

But that's beside the point.

The point is this:

I'm not here to promise you a career in writing if you follow my method and manage to complete a novel in thirty days. A career in writing might not be for you, and I can't change that.

I'm also not here to tell you to hang up your keyboard if you crash and burn on day two. You may find your own way to a career in writing that has nothing to do with my method or any kind of thirty-day novel challenge.

Life is like that sometimes.

And even if my method itself doesn't work for you, you may find some of what I say in this book useful. At least, I hope you do.

Either way, as Kristine Kathryn Rusch told me the first time I took a class with her — **you are responsible for your own career.**

There are no guarantees in life, folks. And you won't find any here either.

NO CHEATING!

I wasn't exactly one of the early adopters of the thirty-day novel challenge. But these days, thanks to the popularity of NaNoWriMo, it's become a much, much bigger thing than it was when I first did it.

Yes. I did say "first." I've gone back and done it a couple of times since. Mostly when I was due to start a novel on November 1st anyway, so why not?

However.

I've noticed that *some* proponents emphasize hitting the word count (50,000 words) over finishing the novel.

These people would have you copy and paste sections multiple times if you're running short. Or even copy and paste individual words over and over and over again, as needed.

Whatever it takes to hit that fifty-thousand word mark, right?

Wrong.

Well. All right. "Wrong" might be a bit harsh. I mean, ultimately, this kind of challenge is done for fun, and it's up to everyone doing it to decide how they want to have their fun.

If they want to copy and paste words or sentences or passages until they hit some magic word-count mark, all so they can call themselves winners and post some kind of sticker to their social media, more power to them.

I don't see the point myself. But my opinion doesn't really enter into it. It's their lives, and they can live them however they want. No skin off my back.

However.

For our purposes — and if you're following my method, I include you in this — that is **CHEATING**.

And it's the *worst* kind of cheating.

It's not cheating the challenge. Because who cares?

It's not cheating your social media followers. Because again, who cares?

It's cheating **you**.

You need to realize something right here and right now.

For our purposes, the thirty-day novel challenge isn't about a word count. Fifty thousand words ... forty thousand words ... a hundred thousand words.

Doesn't. Matter.

What matters is *writing a novel*.

What matters is dedicating yourself to sitting down, day after day (or night after night), and writing the next sentence in the story. And then the next. And then the next. And continuing this way until you finally finish and get to write THE END.

(Note: actually typing the words THE END is optional.)

What matters is starting and *finishing* a story of forty thousand words or more. So that the whole thing is done. Complete. Sitting on your hard drive. Ready for its next step.

(We'll get to the next step later, I promise. Just like we'll get to why I chose forty thousand words in the preceding paragraph. We'll get to all of it.)

Don't cheat yourself.

Don't count words that aren't really part of the story.

Give yourself to the story instead. Lean into it. Love it. Play with it. Let it make you laugh and cry as it reveals itself to you.

Let it be the wild ride that writing a novel is. *That's* what we're here for.

ABOUT WORD COUNTS

All right. So, if hitting fifty thousand words doesn't matter, why care about word counts at all?

It's a reasonable question. And my answer has two parts.

1. The Meaning of Word Count

You can tell a complete story in only a few thousand words. That's what short stories are, after all. Stories of only a few thousand words.

But you're not here to write short stories. After all, the challenge I keep talking about is a thirty-day *novel* challenge. You're here to write a novel.

Which raises the question.

Just how long is a novel?

The problem is, you can get all kinds of answers to that question.

If you go back to the relatively early days of modern publishing, the days of the dime novels and their ilk, a novel was anything over about thirty thousand words.

If you go to the websites of most major publishers these days — which I don't personally recommend, but more on that later — they don't want to talk to you unless your novel is more than eighty or ninety thousand words.

If you go to the awards categories for the different fiction genres (romance, mystery, fantasy, etc.), you'll find numbers as low as twenty-two thousand words (e.g. the Edgar Awards, https://mysterywriters.org/edgars/edgar-award-category-information/).

Not a whole lot of agreement there.

So what number should we pick?

The easy answer here is to just follow the NaNoWriMo guidelines and go with fifty thousand. And that's fine. That's what I did back in 2007, and it's a good total to shoot for.

So why have I been talking about forty thousand words sometimes?

Well, I could tell you that I like the look of it. And I do.

40,000.

I mean, just look at that. Doesn't it look cool?

That's not the real reason, of course.

The real reason is that most of what I write is either science fiction or fantasy, and the Science Fiction and Fantasy Writers of America consider a novel a work of forty thousand words or more.

Mind you, I'm not now, nor have I ever been, a member of SFFWA. But since all the major fantasy and science fiction magazines follow their guidelines regarding story length and professional payment, so do I.

SFFWA says a novel is forty thousand words or more. That's good enough for me.

As such, I'd be a hypocrite if I sat here and said, "I consider anything *I* write that's forty thousand words or longer a novel. But I'm going to make *you* write at least fifty thousand words if you want to call *yours* a novel."

I think we're all hypocrites from time to time. Doesn't mean I *aspire* to be one.

So, far as I'm concerned, if you write a complete story of forty thousand words of more, you've written a novel.

Complete success, in my book. And I wouldn't want you in ashes and sack cloth over the "missing" ten thousand words that probably didn't belong in your story in the first place, or you would have written them.

Stories have natural lengths. I respect that, and I think you should too.

2. The Meaning of Counting Words

There's another reason to worry about word count. You're on the clock. You have a deadline.

Once Day One of your challenge comes around, you only have thirty days to finish your novel. And while I might be flexible about how long your novel needs to be, I'm a stickler for deadlines.

Yeah, yeah, I know. There's a famous writer who spoke of how he loved the "whooshing" sound deadlines made as they flew past.

Personally, I like to think he was joking. Certainly he was known for humor in his writing. But I never met him, so I never got to ask.

And I know. The romantic American image of the tortured artist writer involves lots of struggle, and missing deadline after deadline, but everyone makes allowances because that writer is just *so brilliant*.

Bullshit.

You want to make a living as a writer? Hit your deadlines.

Yeah, maybe you'll miss one once in a while. Life happens. But part of being professional is doing your level best to hit your deadlines. Most of them exist because others are waiting for you to do your part so they can do theirs.

So whether your target is forty thousand words or fifty thousand words, you have thirty days to hit it.

Now, unless you're already conditioned to writing three-to-eight thousand words a day like some of us, that's going to be a stretch.

Count on needing to write every day.

Keeping track of your daily word count helps with that.

You don't have to use the NaNoWriMo website. Goodness knows I never did, back in 2007. I don't think I looked at it once between when I started and when I finished.

What I suggest is using a spreadsheet. Excel, Google Sheets, whatever you like. Thirty numbered rows, with a formula adding up the total at the bottom. Each day, when you're done, put that day's word count in its cell and watch the numbers grow.

If you're going to write fifty thousand words (50,000), you need to average at least 1,667 words a day.

If you're going to write forty thousand words (40,000), you need to average at least 1,334 words a day.

(Yes. I rounded up. Don't want you falling short.)

I strongly suggest keeping track. If you fall behind, you'll know what you need to do to catch up. And hey, if things get tough at some point, you can look back and see how much you've done already.

Never underestimate the power of surveying what you've done. To this day, I keep a spreadsheet that tracks my daily word counts. Gives me a view of what my weeks and months are like, and what all I've accomplished in a given year.

I find it useful. Perhaps you will too.

TOOLS

All right. Before we get into preparations, let's talk about the tools you either will want or may want to help you on your journey.

1. A Word Processor

This one feels self-evident to me, but I figure I better mention it all the same.

Look. You *can* write on a typewriter if you want. If it appeals to you on some deep level, and you feel you absolutely must. Knock yourself out.

If that's you, personally, I think you're being masochistic. Because once you're done, you're still going to need to get all those words into a computer somehow.

Now, you can *try* to just scan in your typewritten manuscript. But you better hope that your software's optical character recognition is *really, really good*.

I consider that a needless gamble.

It's your life, but I strongly suggest you do yourself a favor. Use a word processor.

Doesn't have to be Microsoft Word. You can use WordPerfect,

Google Docs, OpenOffice, LibreOffice, LaTeX or whatever else appeals to you.

The point is that those things exist for a reason. Pick one and run with it.

And hey, if you really must have that typewriter feeling, try a Freewrite by Astrohaus. I've never tried one myself (and I'm not affiliated with them in any way), but I've heard good things. Should split the difference between the look and feel of a typewriter and the benefits of a word processor.

Now, some of you might be thinking of using EverNote or OneNote in place of a word processor.

That wasn't the wind you just heard. It was me, sighing.

Look. All right. Technically those things take word-by-word input. They even have some limited processing abilities. And they do have the advantage of being available on any phone, tablet, or computer.

But if you write a novel in one of those, good luck compiling your manuscript. They're not made to do it. And you're going to have a hard time doing anything with that novel, if you can't compile the manuscript.

Which means turning back to a word processor.

So save yourself time and effort. Use a word processor.

(Note: as I write this, I can hear some of you asking about Scrivener. We'll get to that.)

2. A Notebook

I don't mean a notebook computer here. I mean a pen-and-paper notebook. Possibly spiralbound, but not necessarily.

I know, I know. How 20th century of me. Especially for the guy who just spent whole paragraphs ragging on typewriters. Next thing I'll be talking about using carbons to duplicate your manuscript or something.

Let me explain.

You only have thirty days to write this novel. Which means you're going to want to take advantage of every open opportunity you can find, to keep that novel going.

Back in 2007, when I was doing this for the first time, I kept a notebook with me at all times. And if I got to work a few minutes early, I sat in the parking lot scribbling down a few sentences or paragraphs or pages before I went to my desk.

I did that every time I had a minute here and there. And it got me thousands of words I might have lost otherwise.

Yes, I know. That made sense in 2007. But these days there are these things called smartphones, and so on.

Which is all well and good.

On the other hand, notebooks don't distract you with notifications. They don't tempt you with other apps. They don't require time to power up. They don't give you loading screens, or demand updates during your precious five-minute window.

Five minutes with a notebook and a good pen guarantees you five whole minutes of writing. That isn't necessarily true with a smartphone.

I love my smartphone. And my smartwatch. And my tablet.

And I still have a number of notebooks around my house with all kinds of things scribbled in them, because they were the best way to get ideas down at the time.

And yes, I know. You'll still have to type those words up later. But if you're only using that notebook for short increments instead of trying to write your whole manuscript that way, typing up what you jotted down won't take all that long.

Personally, I found that typing up the day's handwritten words helped kickstart my evening's writing, and made me *more* productive. Not less.

It's up to you. But I think you should consider keeping a notebook handy.

3. A Novel Management Tool

Every tool in this section of the book is optional, except the word processor.

But this tool is even more optional than the others. If that makes sense.

See, it all comes down to how you think, and how you personally can best organize your novel.

The question is, should you write the whole novel in one big file in your word processor? Or should you break it up into smaller chunks?

Now, for one consideration, some word processors get ... finicky as the word counts grow very large. This is less of a problem in the modern era than it was in 2007, but it can still crop up.

In all fairness, though, modern word processors are good enough that that you could probably just write your whole novel in one file just fine.

If that appeals to you.

Now, when I wrote *Telepathy 1A*, I used a different MS Word file for every chapter. These days, I use a different file for every scene. But I made that change when I started using a novel management tool.

So what is a novel management tool?

It's a program that keeps word processing files inside it, in an organized fashion. You can write and edit them just fine, and you can compile the whole manuscript or only part of it. You can even control the formatting of the output to your liking.

I wrote *Telepathy 1A* without a novel management tool just fine, and complied the manuscript myself when I was done.

But shortly after that, I started using Liquid Story Binder XE, and enjoyed the new organizational powers available to me.

These days I use Scrivener, and like it a great deal. There are others, though. Ulysses and Novlr, for example. I haven't tried those two, though. I only list them to give you options to check out.

The advantage of these programs is that you can move scenes and chapters around freely, without having to cut and paste or worry that you've put something in the wrong place.

The whole organization of the novel lies open for you to look at and manipulate, should you need to.

You can also organize your notes *with* your manuscript, but not *as part of* your manuscript.

For example, in my different novel series, each Scrivener book file includes a non-manuscript section full of details about the world, the characters and so forth. What most people would call a "world book" or "story bible."

And in those non-manuscript sections, you can include images, like maps. In my Cavan Oltblood books, for example, I keep reference pictures of the horses my main characters ride.

You can also organize a whole non-manuscript section of the file for your research, If you like.

Now, if you're seeing the almost *literally* endless possibilities here, then likely you're also seeing the downside I want to warn you about.

Scrivener can become a serious time sink. I barely use a tenth of what that program can do, because I don't need more than I'm using. If you have OCD tendencies in your approach to organization, beware this program.

For the sake of completeness, I should point out that Scrivener and its ilk can also serve as your word processor if you want. (Personally, I don't use it that way, but that's my choice.)

Remember, though. These novel management tools are strictly optional. **You do not need them.** It's never been easier to combine multiple word processing files than it is nowadays, so don't feel obligated to seek out yet another program.

I'm just trying to list here all the tools that I think would be useful, depending on how you work as a writer.

4. EverNote, OneNote, or Similar

"Now wait a minute! Didn't you just say—"

Now hold on there.

What I said up above is that I don't think you should use Ever-Note, OneNote and their ilk *as your word processor*.

That doesn't mean they aren't useful.

You may find yourself with some time to write and your smartphone, and you can absolutely jot down a few sentences, paragraphs or pages in that note program for now, and move them to your word processor later.

I mean, if you *can*, you *should* go straight into your word processor. But sometimes that's not an option. And getting more words down is better than not getting those words down.

Better safe than sorry.

Oh. And in case you're wondering. I still think you should carry a notebook, too. There may be times when it's the best tool available for you, and I'd hate for you to miss out.

5. Transcription Software

Personally, I don't like working by dictation. But that's me. I do freely admit, though, that one of the joys of the smartphone era is that we're all carrying pretty darn good audio recorders around.

If you don't have a smartphone and still want to try dictating your novel, digital audio recorders are good and cheap these days. Check 'em out.

However. Once you've recorded all those words on your hike or your drive home from work or wherever, you'll still need to transcribe them into your word processor.

Now, if you want, you can have someone do this for you. If, say, you have a teen with too much time on their hands, for example. (Personally, if you do, I think you should suggest that teen do their own writing. But that's me.)

But getting someone else to do it isn't always practical. And doing it yourself might feel like a time drag, because we're probably not talking about a few sentences or pages here, but a whole day's writing.

This is where transcription software comes in. Dragon Naturally-Speaking is the big kid in the playground, by a fair margin. But it's not the only option by any stretch. Google these days offers a free option that I hear is pretty good, and I bet there are others you could find if you dig around a little.

I've heard there are also transcription services these days that are quite reasonable.

Honestly, though, since this isn't something I do, I don't feel comfortable telling you how to do it.

If you want to try this, you might check out Kevin J. Anderson's book *On Being a Dictator*. He's been writing by dictation for decades, and if anyone could teach you to do it, he could.

WHERE SHOULD YOU WRITE?

One of the romantic images of the modern writer includes that writer sitting in a café, pecking away at the keyboard and guzzling coffee. Or lattes. Or mochas.

Whatever. I'm not a coffee drinker.

In much the same way, I think the total number of instances involving my writing in cafés, over the last five years, could probably be counted on one hand.

I *can* do it. But I don't do it by choice.

I'm happiest, as a writer, when I can sit in my office and write. Just me and the keyboard.

Well, and the occasional visit from one of the cats. They like to make sure I take breaks for my wrists. Or they just happen to have that kind of timing in their quest of attention.

I find that I can write nonfiction with music going, but for fiction, I often prefer silence.

On the other hand, I mentioned before some local writers I know who — when not housebound by a pandemic or something — like getting together at each other's houses to write together.

In silence, mind you. They don't chatter at each other or anything, except during breaks and when they're done for the day.

The writing time is for *writing*.

I love the idea of that. Doesn't work well for me. I feel exposed, which makes me self-conscious, which pulls me out of the story.

Surrounded by strangers doesn't bother me. Surrounded by friends does.

Weird, I know.

Say it with me now — writing is idiosyncratic.

Which brings us to your thirty-day novel challenge.

Homework time.

Over the next week or two, try writing in different locations. See how that does for you. Try crowded places and empty ones. Noisy places, quiet places.

See how you respond. You might surprise yourself.

Although, I have to note, that as I write this book, my nation is mired in a pandemic. Writing in a crowd or any kind of public place is not even in the realm of possibility.

So, for practical matters, you may well be stuck writing at home. That's the way it goes.

Even so. Experiment. Try writing in the kitchen, or the bedroom. Try the deck / balcony / backyard / whatever. Try writing in the car.

See not only what *can* work for you, but what *works best* for you. You'll want to stick to the latter as much as possible, but it's good to know you have options, if you need them.

I mean, yes, I vastly prefer writing at home, at my desk. But I'm really glad to know that I can, if I need to, write in a busy airport.

It's a good thing to know about yourself, and may well come in handy if you stick to writing beyond Day Thirty.

SHOULD YOU TELL ANYONE YOU'RE DOING THIS?

Trying to write a novel in thirty days is a heck of a thing. Especially the first time.

And one piece of advice I've seen bandied about all over the internet — about every kind of big challenge — is how you should tell everyone and their brother what you're doing. That you'll never finish any kind of big and demanding challenge if you don't have people holding you accountable, or cheering you on. That kind of thing.

So.

Is that true?

If you already know your answer...

Now, if you already know the answer to this question, great! Maybe you've used social pressure / encouragement to help you do the Couch-to-5K thing or some other challenge.

Or maybe you've *tried* to use social pressure / encouragement in the past and the result was a steaming pile of failure. Obviously, the answer for you is a big fat no.

Either way, if you already know the answer to this one, congrats!

That's a great thing to know about yourself. Pat yourself on the back, and skip on to the next section with my blessing.

Now, for the rest of you, who *don't* already know your answer...

Should you tell people what you're doing?

Well, honestly — like so very many things in writing — this depends heavily on what kind of writer you are.

The Example of Yours Truly

Let me use myself as an example first.

When I did NaNoWriMo for the first time, I know I told my wife I was doing it. After all, I would have to go to my computer for a couple of hours every night in a way that was unusual for me at the time.

I wanted her to know what was going on.

However. I wasn't telling her so that she'd check up on me, or ask me about my daily word counts, or anything like that.

I wasn't asking her to help keep me working towards my goal. I just wanted her to know what I was doing.

I think she probably asked once or twice how it was going. Honestly, I don't recall. I know that if she did, I never told her much more than "it's going fine" or something along those lines. I didn't talk about plot or characters. I didn't talk about where I was in my word count.

We talked about the novel after I finished. And I know I gave it to her to read.

But that was after I was done. Not during.

There are two reasons for that, and both are specific to my psychology.

The first is that I *hate* having people looking over my shoulder while I'm doing something. Give me a deadline and I'm good. Tell me I have to make regular reports on the way to that deadline and I will tell you...

Well, there would be a number of colorful words involved, none of them would be very pleasant.

I work best when you give me the deadline and get out of my way.

Now, that's true for me because I will only complete a big project if *I* want to do it. I have to have the desire — the motivation — inside me, or I will rebel against doing it.

Heck, the reason I don't play piano to this day is that my mother *made* me practice when I was a kid, instead of finding a way to get me *excited* about practicing.

I don't blame her. That's how she was taught. That's how a lot of kids are taught. I don't respond well to it, though, and the side effects linger.

The second reason — again, specific to me — is that I can't talk about a work in progress or it messes me up.

Heck, I've written a good two dozen novels at this point, but I still have three or four partials on my hard drive that I may never finish. And all because I made the mistake of talking about them.

Telling anyone about a story before the story is finished does something unpleasant to the creative, storytelling part of my mind. I'm not sure exactly *how* that works. Whether it's because my inner storyteller thinks the story must be finished, or because it loses interest, or something else entirely.

But I can't talk about a story until it's done.

So for me, when I'm doing some kind of challenge, I don't say a goddamn word until I've finished it. That's how I did NaNoWriMo back in 2007. That's how I did Couch-to-5K. That's how a completed a challenge to write a short story a week, every week, for a year solid.

Now, that's probably a whole lot more about the inner workings of my mind than you *ever* wanted to know. And I don't blame you.

But I told you all that for a reason. Remember — and I'm sure I'll mention this several more times before we're finished — writing is idiosyncratic.

It's not about how to write a novel. It's figuring out how *you* can write a novel. That's the trick.

For me, if I tried to tell the world what I was doing, it would slam the door on my creativity. Even if I managed to finish, it would be struggle. I'd resent the project. I'd resent everyone who ever mentioned it to me.

So for me, the answer would be a big fat **NO**.

However...

Fine. That's me. What about you?

There's a reason the advice to tell people what you're doing is so popular.

It works for a lot of people.

I'm not one of those people. But you might be. You might be the kind of writer who does a lot better if you have friends (or even online acquaintances) either keeping you accountable or cheering you on.

The question is, *are* you that kind of writer? Or are you more like me?

Neither is better, by the way. Just a reminder. This is all about figuring out what works best *for you.*

The question is, how do you find out which kind of writer you are without screwing yourself up in the process?

Simple.

Try the social pressure thing with something non-writing-related first. Something else you'd like to do. Maybe daily pushups or sit-ups, or running, or something else non-exercise-related.

Some way you can challenge yourself, and get other people involved in either holding you accountable or cheering you on.

Right now, I hope, you're thinking of some kind of challenge along these lines that you can try.

How does that feel? I mean, down in your body.

When you think of reporting daily on your pushups or whatever, do you feel excitement? Does it make you feel eager, to imagine, say, a dozen people in a subreddit cheering on your progress to running your first 5K?

Imagine it. Imagine your friends all coming to you to ask about your progress. Or to congratulate you on hitting your day's goal. Imagine your significant other asking about your progress every night at dinner.

What are the sensations you get when you imagine these things?

See, for me, all the sensations are anxiety. Tension in my shoulders and jaw. Discomfort in my guts. I get anxious and uneasy. My breaths get shorter.

If you find yourself having similar responses to just *imagining* people checking on your progress that way, then don't even bother really trying it. It's not for you, any more than it is for me. Save yourself the headache.

On the other hand, if thinking about these people cheering you on, or eagerly asking about your progress makes you feel excited and enthusiastic, if it makes you eager to get started, then I say try it. That suggests to me that you're the kind of person who'd respond well to it.

In short...

If you don't know, imagine doing it. See how you react physically and emotionally to the scenarios you imagine.

If you react well, go for it. Tell your significant other, your friends, an online forum, whatever group gets your juices going.

If you react with anxiety, I say give this one a pass and go after it on your own.

This is not a small undertaking. Don't make it stressful.

QUICK SUMMARY

I'm going to try to summarize some key points at the end of each section. You might be tempted to just skip most of the text, and read the summaries.

Don't cheat yourself. These summaries are an aid. Not a replacement.

Which brings us to the first point.

1. No Cheating!

Only count words that are actually part of your novel. Not fluff included to hit a magic number.

2. Word Counts

I personally use the SFFWA definition of a novel, which means I consider a novel any completed story of more than forty thousand words. So if you pass that with a complete story by your Day Thirty deadline, I consider your effort a success, even if you don't hit the NaNoWriMo standard of fifty thousand words.

Also, I strongly suggest you keep a running total of your daily word count. You're working with a deadline, and tracking your progress can be a big help.

3. Tools

Word processor. Use one.

I also think you should keep notebooks handy, and have note-taking software available for when either is the best option for getting a few words down in spare moments. But really, you need a word processor.

You might want to use a novel management program like Scrivener, but be aware it's like a time sinkhole for the OCD-inclined. And I consider this even more optional than the other tools.

Except the word processor. You'll want one of those.

If you want to try dictation, cool. But you'll need transcription software, to get your words into your word processor.

Because you'll need a word processor.

Oh. And if I haven't been clear enough here — **use a word processor.**

4. Should You Tell People?

Tough call. I say, imagine doing so and see how it feels, physically and emotionally. If the thought excites you, go for it. If not, avoid it like the plague.

5. The Warning

On the off chance that you *have* decided to only read the summaries, be aware that I'm not offering any promises or guarantees. I'm telling you what worked for me, and how it might work for you.

The rest is up to you.

As multi-multi-multi-award-winning writer Kristine Kathryn Rusch warned me the first time I took a class with her: **You are responsible for your own career.**

CHAPTER TWO

PREPARING YOURSELF

AND NOW, SOME WRITING

ALL RIGHT, FOLKS!

We've got the preliminaries out of the way. Now we can get on to the fun stuff. Actually getting ready to write a novel in thirty days.

So. If you've gotten this far, I imagine you've got your tools ready, you've decided whether or not you're going to tell people, and you're ready to hit that deadline without cheating.

Excellent!

Now it's time to start preparing *you* to write a novel in a month.

I mean, if you decided to run a marathon, you wouldn't just buy the right clothes and shoes, then show up on the day and start running.

At least, I hope you wouldn't. It'd be a terrible thing to do to your body.

Really, you'd have to prepare in advance for something like that.

You'd have to do stretches. Go for walks, then longer walks. You'd have to start running, and run longer and longer distances until you got yourself into shape to not only *attempt* that marathon, but *complete* it.

In much the same way, you'll want to train for your thirty-day novel challenge.

You're going to have to get into the habit of writing every day, so that when we reach Day One, you can hit the ground running.

And that's the whole purpose of this section. To get you ready so that when Day One comes around, you already have momentum on your side. You already have confidence on your side.

You'll be prepped and ready.

And that's the best way to succeed.

Note: You might be tempted to skip this chapter. Especially if you already write on something like a regular basis.

I strongly suggest not skipping. Doing my exercises won't hurt you. And those exercises might have unexpected benefits.

Give them a shot.

HOW THIS IS GOING TO WORK?

I'm giving you this warm-up in three parts. It's the same approach I used back in 2007, and the way I did it then was this:

Part One: August

Part Two: September

Part Three: October

You see how that comes together. By the time November came around, I had just about three months even of daily writing experience. That was a serious boost to both my skills and my confidence, and I think it was a major contributor to completing my novel in twenty-two days.

Now, here's the thing.

The book you're reading is likely to be *published* in September of 2020.

Does this mean that you have to wait until at least 2021 to try my method, if you want to do your thirty-day novel challenge as part of NaNoWriMo?

Well, if you pick this book up in late October, it's true that I can't do much for you, in terms of preparing you by November 1st. (Though you'll still benefit from Chapter 5 and beyond.)

However.

At the end of this chapter, I'll include how to organize these exercises in a condensed timeline. I don't think you'll get as much out of it that way, but it will let you pick up the book in late September or early October, still benefit from some preparation by the time we reach November.

Now. On to the exercises!

THE WARM-UP - PART ONE

The first part of the warm up is pretty simple. This is how it goes. For the next month, this is what I want you to do:

1. **Get to your writing desk every day.**
2. **Write 250 words of new, unrelated fiction. Every day.**

Now that's the short version. Let's take a look at what you need to do in a little more detail.

1. Get to your writing desk every day.

Now, we've already talked about tools, and where you should write. So by now you should have some idea of what "writing desk" means to you.

Whether it's a cozy spot in your kitchen, tucked into the driver's seat of your car, actually sitting at a desk and keyboard, or something else entirely, you need to go there every day.

Every. Day.

Do not skip. Do not let the siren song of other activities call you away. Do not think, "Oh, I've done ten days in a row, I deserve a break."

Every. Day.

Remember. You're preparing yourself to meet a deadline. And that deadline doesn't care if your team is in the playoffs, or that new video game just came out, or the new season of your favorite show is now available for your binging pleasure.

Get to your writing desk. Every. Day.

This is what it takes to be a writer. You need to be able to go to your writing desk no matter what else is going on, and you need to keep producing words.

Now, does this mean that there are no good reasons to miss a day?

Of course there are. You might find yourself too sick to write. Or you might have an accident, or something could happen that shakes you up too much to write.

These things happen, even to professional writers.

But be honest with yourself here.

Is there a *reason* you can't get to your writing desk today? Or do you just *have an excuse* not to go to your writing desk today?

If it's an excuse, get to your desk.

I mean it.

Because, folks, once you start letting yourself make excuses not to write, those excuses will come easier and easier. Then a week will go by without any writing. Then a month.

Then the next thing you know, you think about writing, but you never do any.

It happens. It used to happen to me. Back before I made daily writing a part of my life.

These days, I write five days a week. It would be seven, except that I don't write on weekends so I can have that time with my wife.

But I absolutely could write seven days a week. And I have. And I likely will again at some point.

Going to my writing desk is a joy for me, not a task.

And I want it to become a joy for you too.

But it also needs to be a habit.

See, if I go a few days without writing, I get cranky. I'm much easier to be around when I'm writing. And I am *far* from the only professional writer for whom that's true.

Develop the habit, folks.

Get to that writing desk. Every. Day.

Yes, there will come a point where you could do five days a week like I do. But I didn't start there, and neither should you.

Every. Day.

Don't cheat yourself. Get to your writing desk.

2. Write 250 words of new, unrelated fiction. Every day.

Once Day One rolls around, you'll be trying to write about 1,667 words a day.

(Yes, I know. If you're going for a 40,000-word novel, you only need to his 1,334 words each day. But you won't know when you start out just how long your novel will be. So assume you'll need those extra words, and let the novel tell you if you don't. Worst thing that happens is you finish early.)

This is your first step that direction.

Why two hundred fifty words?

I picked that number because, if you use standard manuscript formatting, two hundred fifty words is about a page.

And yes, I learned my lesson after that first short story rejection, and figured out standard manuscript formatting.

Now, the truth is, exactly how much space two hundred fifty words takes up depends as much on your font choice as it does the fiddly details of your formatting.

But two hundred fifty words is still a good total to shoot for, out of the gate.

Yes, you could decide to start with one hundred. I don't suggest it. See, remember that the goal here isn't hitting a word count, so much as it is telling a story.

If you say that only a hundred words is good enough, you're not giving yourself a chance to actually dig into a character or a situation.

A hundred words is hardly enough space to get down even part of a scene or idea.

I want you to dig into a scene a little bit. To get a feel for a character in a setting. Maybe even with a problem.

Now, for a pro, two hundred and fifty words is hardly enough for throat-clearing. But when you're just starting out, even that much might feel a little daunting.

That's why I say dig into it. Feel your way into the character. The setting. The situation.

You don't need all the answers here. Just let yourself explore. Play. Have fun.

Which brings us to the other half of this requirement.

New, unrelated fiction.

Now, you might write two hundred fifty words about a character on that first day and want to continue that same story the next day.

Don't do that. Not yet.

Take what you wrote on day one and set it aside. Start something entirely different on day two. And then set that aside and write something entirely different on day three.

Play with genres, if you like. Romance or mystery or science fiction or fantasy or historical or whatever. It's only two hundred fifty words. Go nuts.

Play.

The point is, for this exercise, I want you to sit down and write something *new* each day.

This is important, folks. Don't gloss over it.

I mean it.

...

...

Well, hell.

Some of you are thinking of ignoring the "new, unrelated fiction" part. I can *feel* it.

Fine.

Let me give you two good reasons *why* you should do this my way.

First, **pressure.**

If continuing your scene from day one is an option, you might start thinking you *should* be able to continue that scene on day two. And then on day three.

Before you know it, you're putting pressure on yourself to keep that story going. After all, you're training to write a novel, right? Surely you should be able to keep a story going for a few days.

Folks, this is *part one* of the exercise program.

We'll get to finishing stories and writing longer.

We'll get to continuing from the previous day's writing.

We'll get to those things *later*.

Right now, I don't want you feeling the pressure to keep a story going.

Right now, I just want you to get to your desk every day and write something new.

Give yourself that room to *play*. To fling ideas at the page with wild abandon. To *have fun* without any pressure to finish what you start.

Two hundred fifty words.

You can do that.

Now, the second reason. **Ideas.**

Suppose the first time you start doing this daily writing, you manage tell a continuous story day after day and finish a short story a week or two later.

What are you going to do when that story is finished?

You might feel stymied. You've gotten in the habit of writing, but you've gotten in the habit of writing *one story*. And now that story's done.

You might struggle to come up with another idea. You might turn back to that short story. Maybe start revising it.

The next thing you know, time's passed and you haven't kept up your daily writing.

I've seen it happen to people.

The truth is, folks, ideas are the easy part.

We all have a darn near endless stream of ideas to pull from. We just have to let ourselves recognize that.

Part of this exercise is teaching you that you can sit down and write, without knowing in advance what you're going to write.

Ideas are easy. It's the writing part that takes time and effort.

So let yourself play with a new idea every day, for two hundred fifty words.

And don't feel you have to stop after 250 words. Truth is, **two hundred fifty words is your minimum.** If you have some momentum going, feel free to write more. Just don't feel you *have* to.

Do it only because you're having fun, or because you want to see where the scene is going. Preferably both.

Then tomorrow, *set that aside and write something else.*

Oh, and keep all those story starts, folks. Because once you finish your thirty-day-challenge novel, you might want to come back and turn those starts into short stories, or even novels.

I know. I've done it myself.

A NOTE ABOUT IDEAS

All right. What I'd like you to be able to do is sit down every day and just start writing. Just pull an image, or a character, or even a setting out of your head and start going.

I have to admit, though, that this may be difficult for some people.

If you're having problems, chances are, you're pushing. Letting the blank page get to you.

Stop a second.

Stare out the window. Let your mind wander.

If you could be anywhere right now, where would you be? Put a character there and start writing.

What's the place you'd *least* want be right now? Put a character there and start writing.

What's your favorite thing to do?

What do you hate more than anything else?

Who have you always wanted to meet?

These are just a few sample questions, to get the juices flowing. The point is that you can take a character — any kind of character you want — and put them in any situation you want.

Here in the western part of the world, every story starts with a character, in a setting, with a problem.

If you have any one of those things, you can figure out the other two pretty quickly, and start writing.

If none of those things are working for you, here are a couple of other suggestions.

* Search the internet for "writing prompts." There are literally thousands of them out there. Possibly millions. Pick one and go.

* Run an image search for any word, whether as specific as "scorpion" or "gunslinger" or as generic as "romance" or "fantasy." Look over the images that come up. Find one that appeals to you, and start telling the story of that image.

These things should help you get started, for now.

But as you go about your day, start looking for ideas. Odd things you see. Words you hear wrong. Odd images that flit into your head.

Once the creative part of your mind — your inner storyteller — understands that you want story ideas, you'll start finding them all over the place.

Then you'll end up with so many that you know you'll never get to them all.

And maybe you won't.

But it's fun to try.

QUICK CHECK IN

All right. We've reached the end of your first month of daily writing exercises.

How did Part One go for you?

Yes, I realize you can't actually answer me. But I want you to think about the answer to that question, anyway.

In fact, let's break that question down into some specifics.

1. Did you get to your writing desk every day?

If you did, *congratulations!* That's a big step right there. You're already on the road to making writing a habit that will help you immeasurably if you stick with writing in the coming years.

If you didn't, why not?

Did you miss because of *reasons* or *excuses*? (And I went over the difference between these previously. Same definitions here.)

If you missed because of reasons, well, that's life. It happens. Stick with it, and you'll get there. How much did you miss? If a lot, maybe you should start Part One over (possibly using a compressed timeline from the Short on Time section later in this chapter, if you have a specific Day One in mind).

If you missed because of excuses, well, that's on you. Time for a hard question.

Are you sure you want to do this?

If the answer is no, that's all right. That's not a failure. You've attempted something that most people *say* they want a try, but *never will*. You've attempted it. And that's worth congratulations.

And if you've learned that this isn't for you, now you *know* that. You can turn your attention elsewhere, knowing that much more about yourself. And that's a good thing.

Now, if you missed because of excuses, but my previous three paragraphs pissed you off, then think about why that is. Think about why you let excuses drag you away from the keyboard.

If you want to give this another try, go for it. Start Part One over (possibly using a compressed timeline from the Short on Time section later in this chapter, if you have a specific Day One in mind).

2. Did you write at least 250 words of new, unrelated fiction every day?

If you did, *congratulations!* That's terrific. I mean it. You've taken a big step here. You're developing skills and you're developing confidence, and those will stand you in good stead going forward.

If you didn't, why not?

If you gave yourself a lower target, I think you made a mistake. Remember you're preparing to write a novel in thirty days. You're preparing to write to a deadline. You need to average a word count that's more than *six times* what I asked you to do.

If you're shorting yourself now, when your target was only two hundred fifty words, how are you going to hit those higher word counts later?

Personally, I think that if you've been shorting yourself, you should repeat this section (possibly using a compressed timeline from the Short on Time section later in this chapter, if you have a specific Day One in mind).

If you had trouble coming up with new ideas — even after going through all the options in the preceding section — then likely you're asking too much of your ideas.

I've met would-be writers who will never finish anything, because they judge the hell out of every idea they have.

Is this idea good enough?

Is this idea worth my time?

Or the biggest killer of all — *Is this idea truly original?*

Folks, you don't need to come up with an idea that no one anywhere has ever thought of before.

You just need an idea that appeals to *you*.

Let me give you an example.

Suppose you love vampires and really want to write a vampire story.

Well, there are more vampire stories out there in the world — in print, right now — than I even want to think about. I've even contributed a couple myself.

In fact, counting only the novels, there are probably more vampire stories in print right now than there were *total novels in print*, say, when *Dracula* was first published.

So does that mean you shouldn't write a vampire story?

HELL NO!

Go nuts! Write that vampire story. Pour your heart into it and have a blast.

In fact, turn it into a vampire series. And then write a whole set of spinoff series.

If ... that appeals to you.

See, the point isn't coming up with a story idea that no one else has ever had.

The point is *telling your version* of whatever story idea you have.

You could give the exact same story idea to a dozen different professional authors, and do you know how many different stories you'd get?

If you said "a dozen" you'd be close.

If you said "more than a dozen" you'd be closer.

See, sometimes you can turn an idea into a whole novel, or even a series of novels. And yet, known only to you deep down inside, it still didn't come out quite the way you wanted it to.

So you can write that idea all over again as an entirely new story. And that's fine. Your readers will probably love it.

The truth is, ideas are nothing.

Execution is everything.

So let yourself write any idea that comes to mind. Even if it feels silly or cliché or whatever. *Your take* on that idea may breathe new life into it.

And that's worth doing.

So if you've fallen short because you haven't trusted your ideas, you should probably do Part One again (possibly using a compressed timeline from the Short on Time section later in this chapter, if you have a specific Day One in mind).

THE WARM-UP - PART TWO

Excellent! You've finished Part One of the warm-up.

Now. Let's build on your momentum and start stretching you a bit.

This is how Part Two goes:

1. Get to your writing desk every day.
2. For the first seven days, write at least 500 words of new, unrelated fiction. Every day.
3. On day eight, start a short story. At least 500 new words each day until the story is finished.
4. When that story is finished, start another one the next day. At least 500 words.
5. Continue like this until you're close to the end of the month. Then just 500 words of new, unrelated fiction each day to finish the month.

Now that's the short version. Let's take a look at what you need to do in a little more detail.

1. Get to your writing desk every day.

All right. I don't think I really need to go over this one again. You know by now that you need to do this. If you aren't doing it, you're only cheating yourself.

Don't cheat yourself. Get to your writing desk, whatever that phrase means to you.

2. For the first seven days, write at least 500 words of new, unrelated fiction. Every day.

Not much to add here, either. You know by now what I mean by new material, and you should have a way of developing ideas that you'll let yourself play with.

Remember. You want ideas that sound like fun *to you*. Don't worry about what anyone else thinks. This is for you. Play. Have fun.

You're responsible for 500 words a day, now. You're up to a third of what you'll have to produce once Day One comes around.

I know, I know. You're in the habit of 250, so 500 looks big. It's not. Just keep writing the next sentence that makes sense to you. Whatever strikes you as the next thing that needs to happen.

Keep going. You can do it.

And remember. Five hundred is a minimum. You're free to go beyond 500, if you're having fun. But don't feel obligated. Five hundred is enough for now.

Oh, and if you've gone over 500 for, say, three days in a row or something, and then the next day you "only" write 500, *that's still great!*

Doing more than the minimum is cool, when it happens. But don't put pressure on it. The point is having fun with your writing.

Keep this up for a week.

3. On day eight, start a short story. At least 500 new words on that story each day until the story is finished.

All right. Now things get more interesting.

At this point, you have about five weeks of daily writing giving you momentum. And five weeks of new daily ideas, to prove to your-self that you have ideas and that you can do this.

You're now ready to start continuing a story.

So whatever idea you have for day eight of this month, now you get to hang with it. Write your 500 words on day eight. Then come back on day nine and write 500 more. And then 500 more on day ten.

Keep this up until you reach the end of the story.

Don't worry about whether or not your ending is the "right" ending. Just keep the story going until you reach an ending that makes sense to you. Gives you a sense of completion. That makes the story feel finished *to you*.

That's how you know you're done.

And I'll tell you a secret.

If, on the day you finish that story, you don't need 500 words to finish it, that's all right. I won't tell anyone. Finish the story and you're done for the day.

However. If you *feel* like coming up with another idea and writing until you pass 500 words for the day, I think that's even cooler.

Don't feel you have to, though. You'll have finished a short story that day, and that's not nothing.

IF YOU HAVE TROUBLE CONTINUING YOUR STORY:

First of all, relax. There's no pressure on this.

Just write the next sentence. What happens next in the story? What would make sense to have happen?

Still stuck? Dig a little deeper into your viewpoint character. What do they want? What's in their way? Why don't they have what they want right now? What do they need to do next, in trying to reach their goal?

Still stuck? Ask yourself, "What's the worst thing that could happen right now?" And make that happen, and make your character react to it.

Still stuck? Maybe you took a wrong turn. Go back and reread what you already have. You might just realize that you wanted the story to go one way, and it wanted to go another.

And the story is always right about these things. Delete the wrong turn, start there, and keep going.

And above all, just let yourself have fun with the story.

You can do this. I believe in you.

NOTE:

If you finish your first story and there are only a couple of days left in the month, skip step four and go on to step five.

If you needed the *whole rest of the month* to finish this first story, that's just fine. Skip the last two steps here and go on to Part Three. You've more than done what I asked for this month, and you're definitely ready to move on.

Speaking of which...

4. When that story is finished, start another the next day. At least 500 words.

The day after you finish that first short story, start another. (Of course, if you started one after finishing that story last night, cool. Keep going on that story the next day.)

Five hundred words on a new story. You know the drill.

5. Continue like this until you're close to the end of the month. Then just 500 words of new, unrelated fiction each day to finish the month.

Don't worry about starting a second or third or fourth or tenth story if you have a couple of days left in the month. Stick to 500 words of new material each day for the rest of the month, so you won't feel caught in the middle of something when it's time for Part Three.

A NOTE ABOUT STORY

After several weeks of starting stories every day without ever worrying about where those stories were going, you might find yourself feeling a little anxious about continuing a story.

And ending a story? That might feel downright scary.

If you're not having this problem, you can go ahead and skip this section if you like.

But if you're feeling those nerves, let me talk a little bit about story.

See, I keep telling you to relax. That you can tell a story. That you can end a story. That you already know how to do those things.

How can I possibly know that about you?

Because I know you've been absorbing stories all your life.

Movies and television shows and commercials. Videos on YouTube and TikTok and all the other social media out there.

Every book and every short story.

Every time someone told you what they did over the weekend, or on vacation, or over lunch.

Stories are everywhere in human society.

In fact, here in the English-speaking western part of the world, before we can even speak or read, we're introduced to stories starting with the phrase "Once upon a time..." or similar.

In other parts of the world, the words may be different, but people are still telling stories to their children.

And that's not all.

Us human beings, we're creatures who love patterns. Give us a series of random numbers or objects, and we'll find a way to relate them. To connect them. To find common elements or threads.

In other words, to find the story behind them.

So, yeah. You already know how to tell a story.

And you already know how to *end* a story. Because you've already encountered thousands of story endings. Some of them you loved. Some you hated. Some, maybe, you didn't understand.

But every one of those stories and every one of those endings — along with your opinions of them — are still somewhere in your memory.

You may not remember all those things consciously, but believe me. The creative part of your mind has absorbed them.

The creative part of your mind already knows how to start a story, how to continue a story, and how to end a story.

The trick is getting out of the way, and *letting* yourself continue and end that story.

And the key to that trick is relaxing. Don't try to force the story. That way lies madness and disappointment.

On some level, you already know what needs to happen next in your story. So stop stressing. Breathe. Take a walk.

Or take a shower. I find that story problems often "solve themselves" when I'm in the shower, because I allow myself the mental space that the creative part of my mind — my inner storyteller — needs to make itself heard.

I know writers who use naps for the same reason. If they feel stuck, they lie down for fifteen minutes, then get up and go back to their desk because they've just solved their problem.

Note the common thread here?

It's not pounding your head against the keyboard, folks.
Relax.
Let yourself write. Don't *make* yourself write.
You can do this.
I believe in you.

QUICK CHECK IN

All right. We've reached the end of your second month of daily writing exercises.

How did Part Two go for you?

Right, let's get down to specifics.

1. Did you make it to your desk every day?

Yes, I keep harping on this. I think it was Woody Allen who said "80% of success is showing up."

You can't write anything if you don't get to your writing desk.

If you aspire to write novels, you are going to have to do a *lot* of writing.

So you need to get to your writing desk. You need to give yourself the chance to write. To get the words down. You need the habit of writing.

So if you made it to your desk every day and wrote, that's great! Well done!

And if you didn't, well, you need to think about why not. Did you have *reasons* keeping your away? Or did you give in to *excuses*?

If you want to write novels, don't cheat yourself.

Get to your writing desk and get busy.

2. Did you write 500 words every day?

If you did, excellent! Congratulations! Realize that between last month and this month, you've written at least *22,750 words*! That's all fiction that you wrote. And that's pretty darned cool.

Sure, most of that is "just" a collection of story starts. But once you finish your thirty-day novel challenge, you'll have thirty or forty different story starts, and you can turn each of those into something longer.

Now, if you didn't get in your 500 words a day, why not?

I hope it's not about ideas. We've covered that pretty well.

I hope by now that you're not shorting yourself. Day One is getting closer, and you need to be building toward success. Five hundred words is just under a third of what you'll be expected to produce every day once Day One hits, so you're not doing yourself any favors if you hold back.

Dig into the story. Into the character. Five hundred words isn't much, really. So if you're having trouble with that, you need to really let yourself feel what your character is feeling, see what your character is seeing.

Let the words flow. You can do it.

3. Did you finish a short story?

If you did, *fantastic!* You're moving the right direction. Take a moment to acknowledge what you've done. Most people will never write a short story, but you've done that now. And you're still building momentum that will come in handy when Day One comes around.

Way to go!

If you didn't, well, let's talk about why not.

If the end of the month came around and that story is still going, well, I guess that's a good kind of problem to have. I mean, that story's likely over 11,000 words long now, which is heading on toward novelette or novella territory, depending on where it ends.

You know what? If this is the case, take it as a win. Accept my heartfelt congratulations and pat yourself on the back. You're doing just fine. And keep that story going as we continue into the next month.

Now, if you didn't finish a story because you had trouble continuing a story over the course of a few days, that could be a problem. Did you go through my suggestions for how to deal with that? Also, did you read the section before this one?

If you did these things and you're still having trouble continuing a story, or trusting your sense of story, or trusting yourself to find the end of a story, you may need to take a break from this program and figure out what the problem is, and how you can assess it.

My personal suggestion would be to pick up a copy of *Creating Short Fiction* by Damon Knight, and work your way through it. It's a great book, and should help you get out of your own way, and put you in a better position to succeed as a writer.

Then come back and try this book again later.

THE WARM-UP - PART THREE

All right! You've finished Part Two and you're ready to move on to Part Three of the warm-up. That's fantastic!

You're starting to really get your legs under you. Time to start pushing a little more.

If we do this right, you won't just have momentum when Day One comes around. You'll have what a couple of writer friends of mine call "ground effect." For pilots, that's a floating feeling they get when flying close to the ground and benefiting from increased lift and decreased drag.

For us as writers, "ground effect" is the way that habit and momentum can work together to make each day's writing even easier than the day before.

It's pretty darned cool.

So. On to Part Three of our warm-up.

1. **Get to your writing desk every day.**
2. **Write 1,000 words of new fiction every day.**
3. **Start a story on day one, and continue that story every day until it's done.**

4. **Assess how much time you have left, and write appropriately. But keep writing 1,000 words per day.**

Now that's the short version. Let's take a look at what you need to do in a little more detail.

1. Get to your writing desk every day.

Look, folks. You know by now that you need to do this. You know why. If you're still giving in to excuses, and not writing on days you have no *compelling reason* not to write, I can't help you.

2. Write 1,000 words of new fiction every day.

First we doubled from 250 to 500. Now we're doubling again from 500 to 1,000. You can do this. And you're building both your confidence and your momentum toward that 1,667 number you'll need to start hitting once Day One comes around.

You can do this.

Piece of cake.

And remember. One thousand words is your minimum. Feel free to keep going beyond that. Especially if you're having fun.

Personally, I suggest letting yourself stretch more, later in the month. Getting closer and closer to 1,667 every day.

I won't require it of you, but it's a good idea. If you're feeling comfortable and having fun.

But remember — 1,000 words is the minimum, and all I'm asking of you.

3. Start a story on day one, and continue that story every day until it's done.

You've already written at least one short story. Now you can write another. And possibly another after that.

Start a new story on day one of Part Three, and keep at that story — 1,000 words a day, minimum — until that story's finished.

Doesn't matter if the story you're writing now comes in at 3,000 words or 20,000 words. Stay with that story. See where it's going.

Write that story to its end, or until Day One of your challenge rolls around. (We'll talk about that possibility in the coming Quick Check In.)

If you finished Part Two with a story still going, then on day one of Part Three, keep at that story. Finish it. Only difference is that now you're writing 1,000 words a day instead of 500.

Either way, once you finish your story, look at step four.

4. Assess how much time you have left, and write appropriately. But keep writing 1,000 words per day.

When you finish that story you started on day one of Part Three, take a look at where you are on the calendar. If it's still pretty early in the month, start another short story the next day, and write 1,000 words a day at it until you finish that one too.

Then look at the calendar again.

Repeat as needed.

Depending on how many words these stories run, you might write as many as ten this month.

When I did this back in 2007, I only wrote two stories during Part Three of my warm-up, because the second one just ran that long on me.

And that's fine. Feel free to write a story of 20,000 or 25,000 words this month — the technical term for that is novella, in most genres — if that's the story that comes out of you.

Either way, when that story's finished, look at the calendar. If it's getting late in the month, don't stress trying to start and finish another short story.

Just start writing 1,000 words of new material each day, so you keep your momentum going as Day One approaches.

QUICK CHECK IN

Okay, folks. We're coming down to the wire. You've finished your third month of warm-up exercises, and Day One is just around the corner.

I know you're excited to get that novel going. But before we get to that, let's just take a look at how you did with Part Three of our warm-up.

1. Did you make it to your writing desk every day?

You know the drill, folks. If you had an actual compelling reason to miss, then I understand. Of course.

If you just gave in to excuses, well, by this point you're not setting yourself up for success.

I'm holding up my end here, folks. You need to hold up yours. Get to your desk and get writing. Otherwise, what are we doing here?

2. How'd you do with writing 1,000 words a day?

If it was easy, that's great! Well done. You're in good shape for moving on.

If you kept up the pace, but it was a challenge, that's all right. You're stretching yourself. Just remember to keep having fun with the story, and let the words flow.

Don't try to *make* the words flow. You have to find a way to have fun in the story, so you can *let* the words flow. It gets easier then.

If you fell short, why?

If it's a physical reason, if actually typing that many words is diffi-cult for you, then you need to find a way to address that. You might look into dictation and using transcription software, as I talked about back in the Tools section.

Don't mess with your health, folks. If something physical kept you from writing a thousand words a day, be honest about it. Do you need to stop this program for right now? Do you need to see a doctor? Possibly an occupational therapist?

Consult professionals. Treat your body right.

If you're fine physically, but you still had trouble managing to keep writing 1,000 words every day, you need to consider why that is.

That kind of word count takes many writers, even professionals, about an hour. If the problem is that you can't find that much time every day, then you have to find a way to make that time.

Get up earlier. Go to bed later. Steal time from some other activity.

If you want to write novels, you have to commit to giving yourself time to write.

If it's the writing itself that's a problem — if keeping up the pace of a thousand words a day — is daunting, then stop and take a breath.

Writing is a weird thing to do. Psychologically, I mean. It's easy to develop little ways to trip yourself up and keep yourself from writing. Making the words important, or stressing over one aspect of the story or another.

If these are the kinds of problems you're having, slow down.

Realize that these are just stories. No one is going to come to your house with a baseball bat if they don't like your story.

You don't need to write the greatest story the world has ever seen. You just need to tell the story you want to tell.

In fact, you know what the worst novel ever written is?

It's a completed novel!

Which means that the "worst" novel ever written is infinitely better than every single unfinished "masterpiece" ever begun and abandoned.

Don't worry about whether or not your story is "good enough." Writers are always the worst judges of our own work anyway.

All you need to do is relax and have fun. Tell the story you want to tell, the best way you can.

You can do it.

Keep going.

3. Did you finish one or more stories?

If you did, that's terrific! That's more completed stories for you, and we'll talk about what to do with those stories later.

If not, why not?

Did you manage to finish the month with that first story still going?

Whuf.

All right.

Hate to say it, but you'll need to set that story aside for your thirty-day novel challenge. You can't use it, because you started it before Day One. But you can come back to it after Day Thirty and finish it then. And I hope you do.

If you never let yourself finish a story, just abandoned stories incomplete and started new material the next day, we have a problem.

See, you need to finish what you start. You're training to finish a novel, and if you're not letting yourself finish a short story, that's only going to get worse.

Look back at what I said above, for those who had trouble writing 1,000 a day. See if any of that applies to you.

If not, well, you might not be ready for a thirty-day novel challenge. If you're unwilling to finish a short story, you're heading for trouble, trying to finish a novel.

If this is you, you might want to walk away from the thirty-day novel challenge for now. Go read *Creating Short Fiction* by Damon Knight and work through his exercises. That should help you trust yourself to finish stories.

Then come back, go through the warm-ups again, and hit the ground running for that thirty-day novel challenge.

SHORT ON TIME?

I've been writing this book on the assumption that — as I did back in 2007 — you made the decision early in the year that you would attempt NaNoWriMo. Thus, having lots and lots of time to prepare for it.

So much time that you could spend three months doing exercises.

But maybe that's not your situation.

Maybe you got this book with only a month or two to go before November 1st. Or maybe even just a few weeks.

NOTE: if you're starting this book with only a few *days* before NaNoWriMo starts, you're not going to have time to go through the exercises this year. If this is the case, I hope reading the book still helps you.

Now, if you're short on prep time, the most honest advice I can give you is forget about November 1st this year. Just pick a different day for Day One of your thirty-day novel challenge, and give yourself time to work through the exercises.

They're worth it.

But some of you won't want to do that. Some of you will just want to do short versions of the exercises, and start on November 1st — or whatever Day One you'd chosen — as you originally planned.

So, if that's you, and you *do* have at least a couple of weeks to work with, you may be looking at the warm-up exercises and asking how you can use them.

This is what you could do.

1. **Count the days between now and November 1ˢᵗ (or whatever Day One you chose).**
2. **Spend half those days on Part One of the warm-up.**
3. **Spend half the remaining days on Part Two of the warm-up.**
4. **Spend the final days on Part Three.**

Let me explain that in a little more detail.

1. Count the days between now and November 1ˢᵗ (or whatever Day One you chose).

Include today, if you can. You're going to want to get started as soon as possible. Remember that you *should* include the day before your challenge starts (e.g. October 31ˢᵗ), but *not* Day One (e.g. November 1ˢᵗ). After all, you'll be starting your novel on Day One.

If there's an odd number of days, give the spare day to Part One. Just to be safe.

2. Spend half those days on Part One of the warm-up.

This one is pretty straightforward, since you're doing the same thing every day. Two hundred fifty words of new, unrelated fiction.

3. Spend half the remaining days on Part Two of the warm-up.

This is a little different. Because you're short on time, start a short story on day one of Part Two, and continue that story until you finish it.

If you finish that short story before you've finished Part Two, start another.

Either way, make sure you're writing your 500 words each day.

4. Spend the final days on Part Three.

Following a compressed timeline, you likely have a story going when you reach day one of Part Three. That's fine. If so, just continue that story, only now you're writing 1,000 words a day.

If you finished a short story at the end of Part Two, start another one on day one of Part Three, and keep at it every day until you either finish it or reach Day One.

If that story is still going when you're done writing for the day on the day before your challenge starts, just set it aside for now. Start your novel on Day One, and come back to your short story after you've finished your novel.

If you follow the program this way, the effect should snowball for you, and you should still have a good amount of momentum carrying you into your thirty-day novel challenge.

You should do the whole program if you can, though. The extended amount of practice and habit-building would stand you in good stead.

QUICK SUMMARY

Once more, I'm going to remind you. These summaries are intended as an aid. Not a replacement for reading the whole chapter. I cover a lot more in those chapters than I'll touch on in these summaries.

Don't cheat yourself.

All right, then.

1. Time Frame

I wrote this based on my original program, which allowed for three months of exercises before starting your thirty-day novel challenge. If you don't have that much time, for some reason, that's all right. We can make this work for you.

2. The Warm-Up Part One

Get to your writing desk every day and write at least 250 words of new fiction, unrelated to anything you've written so far. Write more if you like, but make sure you get your 250 words each day.

3. The Warm-Up Part Two

Get to your desk every day and write at least 500 words of new fiction. For the first week, write unrelated stuff each day. Brand new starts. After that, start and finish short stories for the rest of the month, at a rate of at least 500 words a day.

4. The Warm-Up Part Three

Get to your desk every day and write at least 1,000 words of new fiction. Start and finish short stories until you get close to the end of the month. Then just stick to new story starts each day, continuing to write 1,000 words every day.

5. About Ideas

If you get stuck when coming up with ideas, I give you some suggestions for dealing with that. I'm not going to repeat them here, though. If I did this would no longer be a *quick* summary.

6. About Story

If you find yourself stressing out about what comes next in your story, relax. Breathe. Take a walk or a shower. And allow yourself to realize that you've been absorbing stories every day for your whole life.

7. Short on Time?

If you don't have enough time before Day One to do all the exercises the way they were meant to be done, you can abbreviate the process.

Take the number of days you do have and divide that number in two. Spend that many days on Part One of the warm-up.

Divide the number of remaining days by two. Spend that many days on Part Two of the warm-up.

Spend the remaining days on Part Three.

Done this way, your momentum should snowball and still prepare you for the amount of writing you'll have to do during your thirty-day novel challenge.

But you really should do the whole exercise program, if you can.

CHAPTER THREE

WRITING THAT NOVEL

TIME TO WRITE A NOVEL!

HERE WE GO, FOLKS! THE MAIN EVENT. THIS IS WHAT YOU'RE HERE FOR.

It's time to take up that challenge, and write a novel in thirty days!

You've got your tools.

You've done your prep work.

You're ready to start writing that novel.

You know what more you need from me for this part?

Nothing.

That's right. That's what I said. Nothing.

If you've come this far, you've already got everything you need to write a novel. You've got the daily writing practice. You've got the habit of writing more than a thousand words a day. You know how to continue a story from one day into the next, and how to keep going until you reach the end of the story.

That's everything you really need.

So when Day One comes around, just head to your writing desk, grab an idea, and go.

And then just keep at it. Get to your writing desk day after day. Hit your word count. Keep the story moving.

You can do this.

Now, it might be that you don't believe this is everything you need. In fact, I think I can feel a couple of your questions, which means you must be thinking them pretty darned loudly.

So I'll cover those in just a moment.

But I want to repeat again, for emphasis.

You've got your tools.

You've done your prep work.

You're ready to start writing your novel.

You've got this.

See you on the other side.

BUT, A WHOLE NOVEL?

Right now, some of you might be stressing out because I've had you writing short stories, and now you're supposed to write a novel.

Well, if you're stressed out at the moment, then first of all, take a breath. Then another. In fact, sit back, put one hand low on your stomach, and take a deep breath that expands your belly. Then let that breath out slowly.

Deep breathing is great for stress reduction.

Please understand, I'm not being flippant or sarcastic about that.

I know what it's like to have my nerves kicking into overdrive when it comes to considering a big project. Right now there's a big, sprawling series that I really want to write, that also scares the hell out of me because of the ways it's going to push me as a writer.

And whenever that fear hits me, the first thing I do is stop what I'm doing and take deep, slow breaths until I've calmed down.

So I'm not asking you to do anything I don't do myself on a regular basis. I'm a firm believer in deep breathing.

Now, then.

Let's talk about what I've really been training you to do for the last three months.

I've been training you to decide in advance what you were going to do at your writing desk, so you could then sit down and do just that.

And that's exactly what you've done for the last three months (or whatever abbreviated time you've had).

You've gone to your desk with a plan. And executed that plan. Day after day after day.

This isn't any different. Only the goal is different.

On Day One, you're going to sit down, pluck an idea from the aether — as you've done dozens of times already — and start writing.

The only difference this time is that you *intend* to write a novel, instead of a short story.

And your inner storyteller understands that intention.

You've been letting your inner storyteller play for weeks now. Letting it stretch.

Now you're just asking it to give you a novel.

And your inner storyteller *absolutely* knows what that means.

After all, you've already read plenty of novels. Maybe hundreds. Maybe even thousands.

So believe me when I tell you that when you sit down *intending* to write a novel — if you've done your prep work — you absolutely are ready to write that novel.

Just relax, and *let* the words flow. Don't try to *make* them flow. The key here lies in having fun with the story. Really dig into it. Get into your characters' heads. Live with them. Breath with them. Strive with them.

Suffer in their failures and exalt in their successes.

Throw yourself into writing your novel with wild abandon.

Your inner storyteller will handle the rest.

NOTE: IF YOU DON'T READ NOVELS

I hate to even mention this, but it occurs to me that some of you may have read what I said a few paragraphs back and said, "But I don't read novels."

Pardon me while I sigh.

Folks, if you don't read novels, why are you trying to write them?

Seriously, it's like saying you want to play guitar, but you only ever listen to piano music.

If you want to play guitar, you need to listen to guitarists. And if you want to write novels, you need to read novels.

I could go on about this, but I'm not going to. You're either going to believe me now, or you'll find out the hard way that I'm right.

Reading, folks. There's no substitute for it.

WHAT ABOUT OUTLINING?

Some of you may have noticed that I've never said anything about outlining.

Ah, outlines.

Don't like 'em.

Don't use 'em.

Wouldn't have 'em in my house.

All right. I admit. That was pretty flippant of me.

More seriously, I am a major proponent of what some would call "discovery writing." Personally, I prefer the term that I believe was coined by Dean Wesley Smith: "writing into the dark."

I've written more than two dozen novels. Of those, exactly one had anything that could *remotely* be construed as an outline. Because a class required it of me in my MFA program.

I threw that tiny, pathetic excuse for an outline out when it came time to write the novel. Didn't look at it once.

Back when I was working with an agent — something I don't recommend by the way — I outlined two sequels to the novel we were trying to sell, in case a publisher asked for them.

I've never written those novels, and I'm not likely to. Writing the outlines stole all the joy of writing from those stories. Those sequels *may* happen someday, when I get to the point that I can think of them without remembering their outlines.

Then again, those stories may never happen. I have too many others to write. Tough to say.

And that's not all.

In my early days as a writer, even though I didn't outline, I used to require myself to have some idea where a story was going when I started. I thought I needed to know the ending, or at least have a good idea about it.

Or if not the ending, at least a coming turning point. Something like that. I'm not sure I recall exactly how that worked, and I'm not sure I want to.

Because the truth is, that approach was holding me back.

When I learned to go of where the story was going, everything I wrote got better.

My stories got *more* complicated, not less. My characters got more believable and involving.

See, this goes back to something I've talked about before.

The creative part of your mind. Your inner storyteller. It knows more about writing than your conscious mind could ever *hope* to know.

I'm not kidding here, folks. In fact, here's a fresh example.

I just finished writing a novel of some 160,000 words, only to find out — when I looked at the beginning again — that things I was writing late in the book tied perfectly into things that had been set up in the earlier parts of the book.

Consciously I had no idea that was happening.

But the deeper part of my mind, my storytelling brain, it knew what it was doing from page one.

Why am I telling you all this?

Because the creative, storytelling part of *your* mind knows what it's doing too.

Trust it.

Trust your own creativity.

Trust your inner storyteller.

That part of your mind will respond to your trust, and tell a kickass story.

You can do this.

If this idea just makes you too nervous, try reading Dean Wesley Smith's book on the topic. The title, unsurprisingly enough, is *Writing into the Dark*. Dean should be able to help you work through your fears and get started having more fun with your writing.

If, at this point, you still feel the need to outline, I can't stop you. That's up to you.

I can't help you with your outline, though. I wouldn't know where to start, and I'm happier that way.

A NOTE ABOUT MESSY WRITING

I went back and forth about whether or not to include this topic. But really, I think I need to address it.

There is a trend among some writers — and I've seen it bandied about especially when it comes to challenges like this one — to say that the first draft is "just to get the ideas down." Or "the roughest of rough drafts" or some other such thing.

These people seem to espouse "writing messy." Just writing carelessly, really. Wantonly making mistakes all over the place. Maybe putting XXXXXXX wherever there's a word they're not sure of, or [BIG FIGHT SCENE HERE] if they don't feel "ready" to write that scene, and so on.

The idea appears to be that the first draft can be as ugly and messy as it "needs to be" in order to "get it finished," with the "real work" then being to go back and "fix" it.

You may have noticed that I'm using a whole lot of quotations marks in this section. There's a reason for that.

I think it's a load of crap.

I think that if you write that way, you're setting yourself up for failure, not success.

By now you should know that I'm all about preparation and

intention. I firmly believe that what you accomplish when you sit down to write depends greatly on a) how you've prepared, and b) what your intentions are.

If you "allow" yourself to write a complete wreck of a first draft with the intention of "fixing" it later, you're telling your inner storyteller that what you're doing right now doesn't matter.

That is the exact opposite of what I want you to do.

I want you to write the best novel you can write. And part of that is making what you do at your writing desk *mean* something.

And that means setting out to write your novel as best you can. The first time.

So how do you do that?

Simple.

First of all, each day, before you go to your writing desk, *set your intention to write the best novel you can write.*

Intention, folks.

(If you're not sure what I mean about setting your intention, check out the next section. I thought about explaining it here, but figured it really needed its own section.)

Then, when it comes to your daily writing, start by reading over what you wrote yesterday. Fix any mistakes you catch as you read.

When you reach the end of yesterday's writing, keep going. Write the next sentence and start building toward your day's word count.

If you do this every day, when you finish your novel you'll have a solid first draft. And the more you write this way, the cleaner your first drafts will get.

Yes, typos will still creep in. They're all but inevitable.

But if your *intention* is to write clean, you won't have nearly as many mistakes. And more importantly, your *stories* will be better.

In other words, you might have some little things in the *manuscript* to fix later, but your *story* will come out right. And that's what really matters.

Intend to write the best novel you can.

Intend to write as cleanly as possible.

These intentions will pay vast dividends over time.

A NOTE ABOUT SETTING INTENTION

All right. I've been using the word "intention" a whole lot. Haven't I?

You might be wondering what I mean by "setting your intention" and how it's done.

Well, first of all — and I can't say this strongly enough — I *don't* mean girding yourself for a fight, or focusing hard on what you want to do.

Setting your intention isn't about how *hard* you think about what you want. And it's not about reminding yourself over and over what you're doing.

The truth is, once you've set your intention to do something, you don't really need to consciously think about it again.

So what, then, is setting your intention?

Setting your intention is just *deciding* in advance what you're going to do, *and meaning it*.

That's all there really is to it.

Let me give you a non-writing example.

Suppose you set your intention to go running on Saturday. The idea occurs to you earlier in the week. Maybe as early as Sunday, maybe as late as Friday night.

Either way, you like the idea. You decide that you'll do it. You'll go running on Saturday.

Once you've made that decision — and *meant it*, not just contemplating an idle fantasy — part of your mind will put "running on Saturday" on your internal to-do list.

When Saturday comes around, you'll get an itch to go running. And if you don't follow through the first time you get the itch, it'll likely recur periodically throughout the day until you either go running, or specifically don't.

If you don't, you'll likely feel disappointed in yourself. But if you do, you're likely to feel a sense of accomplishment in doing what you set out to do.

And after that first Saturday's running, you may decide that you like it. You may set a new intention to go running the next Saturday. Then you may set your intention to go running every Saturday.

Actually, that brings up a point that I really should cover.

Your intention has to be believable to you.

Now, I consider that part of "meaning it." But I'm going to call it out for clarity.

If you're someone who has never once gone running, setting your intention to start running every day is too big. You won't believe it, deep down, because it's too big a transition from what you know.

That's why you set your intention to go running *once*.

Then after you succeed, you set your intention to go running *again*.

Then, once you've succeeded, you set your intention to go running *regularly*.

You build towards your goal by setting smaller intentions, accomplishing those intentions, and then setting larger intentions.

Some of you, right now, might be noticing that this is exactly how I've been training you to write.

I started you with setting your intention to get to your writing desk every day.

And I had you set your intention to hit a small word count every day. Then bigger and bigger word counts.

After you got used to that, I had you set your intention to continuing stories, and finishing them.

I had you do a lot of that before you got to the point of trying to write a novel. So you could build on your successes and prepare yourself mentally to succeed at writing a novel.

In other words, folks, if you've gotten to this point, *you already know that this works.*

In Conclusion

It's a small thing, really, setting your intention.

It's just deciding in advance what you're going to do, and meaning that decision.

Don't underestimate the importance of that second part.

It's not enough to decide to do something if you know, deep down, that you don't mean it.

That's all right, though. If you've been doing your exercises, then you've already been developing experience at setting your intention and following through.

Now you already know that you're going to set your intention to start and continue a novel when you get to your writing desk. And you already know that the deeper part of your mind will take that seriously.

And if you set that intention to *write the best novel you can write —* the deeper part of your mind will take it from there.

QUICK SUMMARY

This is kind of a weird chapter to write a summary for. So I don't think I'll bother with a numbered list. In a nutshell, this is what we covered:

You're ready to write your novel.

I'm not kidding. You're ready.

No, you don't need an outline.

You just need your sincere intention.

And last but not least...

Don't write a messy first draft. Focus on writing the best novel you can write, *the first time*.

CHAPTER FOUR

FINISHING UP

HOW'D IT GO?

ALL RIGHT, FOLKS. IF YOU'RE READING THIS, I'M ASSUMING THAT YOUR thirty-day novel challenge is over. Or at least, over for you. Either your time is up, or you finished early.

So how did you do?

Did you finish your novel?

If you did, **congratulations!** That's fantastic. Well done. You've accomplished something that most people only dream of. No matter what happens from here, no one can ever take that accomplishment away from you. Skip on ahead to the section called If You Finished Your Novel.

If you didn't finish your novel, that's all right. The attempt alone is a heck of thing, and worthy of congratulations in and of itself. You put yourself out there. Most people wouldn't have the guts to take that risk. Go on to the next section, If You Didn't Finish, and let's look at where you stand.

IF YOU DIDN'T FINISH

All right. So, you ran out of time and your novel isn't finished. That's all right, folks. It's not the end of the world, by any stretch.

Remember something I told you earlier. I know a lot of writers who got their start without any kind of thirty-day novel challenge. Writing a novel in a month isn't the kind of challenge that works for everyone.

So falling short doesn't mean you can't write novels if you want to.

But I'm getting ahead of myself.

Let's look at *why* you didn't finish your novel.

1. Did you hit your daily word count?

Did you get to your desk every day and write your 1,667 words or more?

If you did, good job! Go on to the next question.

If you didn't, why not?

Did you have a *compelling reason* not to write? Or did you have an *excuse*?

If you had some big life event — for example, death in the family or major illness for you or a close loved one — then *do not count this as a failure.*

Don't beat yourself up over it. I've beaten myself up over not writing at times like that, and I can tell you from personal experience that it's not fair, and it's not productive.

Give yourself a break.

Try the challenge again when you're ready, whether it's November or not. You can even repeat the warm-up exercises first, to get your momentum going again.

On the other hand...

If the siren song of video games, television, parties or other activities pulled you away and "kept you" from writing, then maybe this gig isn't for you.

There's no shame in that. Lots of people aren't writers. And they find all kinds of ways to fill their time.

Now, if the preceding paragraph pissed you off, because you consider yourself a writer, then ask yourself this.

"If you're a writer, why didn't you write?"

Thinking about writing isn't writing. Plotting isn't writing. World-building isn't writing. Lots and lots of things aren't writing.

Putting together strings of words to form sentences and paragraphs, scenes and chapters, that tell a larger story — that's writing. (Specifically, writing fiction. Which is what we're talking about.)

If you're thinking of trying to make a go of a career in novel writing, realize that you're going to have to do a *whole lot* of writing.

That's a whole lot of time when you're *not* doing other things, like playing video games, going to parties, watching movies / shows / et cetera.

So be honest with yourself here. Is writing really what you'd rather be doing? Or would you rather be doing something else?

If you think your answer really is writing, that's fine. Take a little time, figure out *why* you let yourself get so distracted that you didn't finish your novel, and try again. Maybe starting January 1st and finishing on January 30th.

2. Did you hit a roadblock in your story?

Did you not finish because you got to a point in your novel where you just could not figure out what happens next?

If this happened, did you go back to the section in Part Two where I talk about what to do if you have trouble continuing your story?

If you went through my suggestions there and you still felt blocked and couldn't keep going, then the problem likely is one of confidence.

This kind of block tends to come up when you don't trust your inner storyteller to keep the story moving. When you try to force the story to go one way when it wants to go another. Or when you try to figure out where the story is going, and your guess doesn't match what your inner storyteller has in mind.

Either way, it's an attempt to control the creative process. Which is, by its nature, a force that resists such controls.

I've mentioned the book before, and I'll mention it again here. *Creating Short Fiction* by Damon Knight. Yes, I know. That's a book about writing short stories, and you want to write novels.

Nevertheless. Working through that book can help you develop confidence in the creative part of your mind. And it's that confidence you need, to trust your inner storyteller and let it finish the stories you write.

I say you work through Damon Knight's book, then come back, maybe repeat the warm-up exercises, and give the thirty-day novel challenge another go.

3. Did you just run out of time?

Did you not finish because it's past your deadline and the novel is still going? More than 50,000 words and counting?

All right. Tell you a secret.

That's not a failure at all.

I consider this a qualified success. And I'm only qualifying it because you're not done yet.

Don't give up. Keep going. Get to your desk every day and keep writing that novel. Keep writing 1,667 words or more every day, day in and day out, until you finish the whole novel. However long it is. However long the process takes.

You can do this.

All right. Right now I can hear some of you complaining. After all, I made a big deal about hitting your deadlines. And here, you've blown right past your deadline. Maybe it even made a whooshing sound. I don't know. I wasn't there.

Here's the thing, though.

This is your first novel. Give yourself a break.

The creative part of your mind is telling a novel-length story, and that's a total success in my book. (As long as you stay with it and finish the novel.)

Yes, you missed your deadline. But you had no way to know in advance that you were writing a novel that would run 80,000 words or 100,000 words or even 60,000 words.

We planned for you to hit 50,000 words, and that's what we prepared you for. That your inner storyteller felt comfortable enough to dig in and tell an even longer story is not a failure. It's a success.

So long as you finish that story.

So.

Back to your writing desk with you.

IF YOU DID FINISH

You finished your novel?

CONGRATULATIONS!

That's terrific.

Seriously. Pat yourself on the back, buy yourself a treat or whatever. You've accomplished something big, and you should stop and recognize that.

So now what?

Ah, that's the real question, isn't it?

Now, there's a lot to that question, and most of it will come up in the next chapter.

Right now, let's just focus on what to do with this novel you've just written.

Actually, no. Let's start by talking about what I *don't* want you to do. Because I can tell you right now that there are hundreds or thousands of people online chattering about exactly what you should do with your novel manuscript.

Most of them have never written *one* novel, let alone several. I'm talking about the agents and self-proclaimed "story doctors" or "content editors" or whatever the hell they're calling themselves these days.

Look.

Whatever you think of me, if you take nothing else away from this book, I implore you to take this one piece of advice:

If you want to build a career, look get your advice from people who are further down the road you want to follow.

I study under mentors who have sold millions of books over the course of decades.

I consider myself qualified to write *this* book, because I'm showing you *what I did*. I wrote that thirty-day challenge novel. Since then I've gone on to write about two dozen more, and I'm constantly writing new stories.

If you're reading this, chances are good that I'm further down the road than you are.

So if you want to ignore my advice from here on out, that's fine. It's your choice. But if so, I strongly suggest that you look to someone even further down the road than I am, and see what *they* have to tell you.

But hey. It's your career. And as I mentioned previously, you're the one responsible for it.

Now then.

What don't I want you to do?

1. Don't turn around and rewrite your novel.

This is a trap, folks, for more than one reason.

First, once you start the rewriting game, it's easy to never stop. To just keep rewriting that one story until it's "perfect."

No such thing as perfect, folks. No story is *ever* perfect.

And worse, while you're "polishing" that novel, odds are good that it's stealing all your writing time. Which means you aren't writing any new stories. And if you want a career at this, you need to keep writing new stories.

You've finished that novel. Let it go.

Second, once you start picking at your novel, you'll end up "polishing" away all the little distinctive elements that make it worth reading.

Those distinctive elements are called "voice." And voice is what makes writers stand out. Voice draws readers.

In fact, I once sold a story to a well-known editor who was sitting on a panel, listening while five other professional editors trashed that story. When it was her turn to talk, she said, "I saw the things they're talking about and I *don't care*. Voice trumps everything. I love this story and I'm buying it."

Trust your inner storyteller. Don't mess with the story.

2. Don't send your novel to an agent.

All right. This is a much bigger issue than I can really go into. But the core idea here is that you don't need an agent. I could go into a number of reasons why, but because of space considerations, I'm going to stick to one.

Remember, an agent's ultimate priority is *their* career, not yours. Their priorities for *themselves* will color the actions they take — or don't take — on your behalf. And they will judge every decision you make by how it affects *them*.

It's good business, maybe, but it's not a partnership you need.

If you want to read more about agents, I suggest looking into Kristine Kathryn Rusch's blog, www.kriswrites.com. She covers the subject very well.

3. Don't post your novel text on a website.

Hmmm. As I write this it's 2020, and I'm not sure whether or not WattPad (or whatever exactly it was called) is still a thing.

Either way, do yourself a favor. Don't just post the whole text of your first novel somewhere online. Not if you want to build a career as a writer.

Two major reasons for this.

First, for those of you who want to consider working with a big publisher — and I suspect that some of you want this — they'll run screaming from you. All right, possibly not literally screaming, but they'll consider your novel "already published." And likely won't be interested.

Second, if you want to go the indie publishing route, the retail stores like Amazon may pull your book down if they find the whole text available to read for free online. Or you may have to prove you wrote it. Either of which is a hassle you don't need.

Note: There are perfectly reasonable people who disagree with me on this one. But if you decide to go ahead and post your book online, I ask only one thing of you first. Do your research. Dig around online. Find out who is doing it, when they've done it, and what happened when they did.

And don't forget to notice *when* they did it. Things that worked well five or ten years ago don't work at all anymore.

Do your research.

Note 2: All right. I just remembered. Technically speaking, I posted a whole novel to my website once, as an experiment. I serialized it over the course of about two months as a series of blog posts.

However.

This was not my first novel. It was about my ... nineteenth maybe? Something like that. Also, I didn't just post the text. Serializing it the way I did broke it into chunks that avoided a number of issues.

What's more, the book was already available for sale at this point, and every posted chapter included links, so people could buy the book there and then rather than wait for the next chapter.

In other words, I didn't just throw the book up on a website. I did my research, made a plan, and executed the plan.

So if you want to do something like this, do your research first. Make a plan. Know what you're doing. Be smart about it.

4. Don't throw it all your friends and beg for their opinions.

Opinions can be dangerous. Especially at this stage. If one friend says they don't like a scene, you may find yourself fretting about it. Or worse, going in and making changes that your well-meaning friends recommend.

And what if a different friend talks about how much they *liked* that same scene? Who's right? How do you decide?

There's a right way and a wrong way to solicit feedback. We'll talk about the right way soon. But this is the wrong way. Don't do it to your friends, or your novel. Or yourself, for that matter.

5. Don't give it to your critique group!

Actually, I'll go a step further. If you're part of a critique group, quit.

Yeah, I know. Sounds severe. But the truth is, critique groups don't help you get better. If anything, they drag everyone down to the quality of the worst writer in the group.

The reason for this is that everyone goes through everyone's stories and "critiques" them. In other words, they read with the intention of finding faults to point out.

And you know how intentions work. They *will* find flaws, whether those flaws are really there or not.

Plus, most of these people are likely beginning writers, who wouldn't know a real story fault from a hole in the ground.

They'll pick at little nothings in the grammar, even though those little nothings are part of what makes your voice great. Or they'll take little story details they don't like, even though those little story details set your tale apart from the crowd.

And as for story faults, their idea of a story fault is anyplace the story does something *they* wouldn't have done if they were writing it.

Let me give you an example from the last story I ever handed to a critique group.

One guy bitched that my *fantasy world* had tomatoes, because tomatoes didn't exist in Europe until they were imported from America.

I kid you not.

Another complained that I had names derived from Germanic languages and Celtic languages in the same story.

Another complained that my swordswoman was "too strong," and shouldn't be able to compete with men on an equal footing.

Yeah.

I didn't change any of that, and I didn't go back to that group. Or any other.

Oh, and if you think that sounds like a bad example, that was actually from the best critique group I was ever part of. And I could find you countless examples from others, because back in the day I was part of several over the course of a few years. And I still have all those notes. Someplace.

When you're part of a critique group, you're expected to take the critiques seriously. As though the people around you were experts, when they likely don't have any more publishing experience than you do. Or if they do, not *much* more.

Remember. If you want a career in writing, take advice from people who are further down the road you want to follow. Not people who are behind you. Not people who are next to you. People who are further down the road.

Critique groups won't help you tell *your* stories. They won't help you tell *better* stories. They *will* hurt your confidence.

Maybe you think your critique group is different. I sincerely doubt it, but it's your life, and your career. Your responsibility, not mine.

Do what you think is best. But don't say you weren't warned.

All right.

I think I've covered the big danger signs.

Let's move on now to things you *should* do, or at least consider doing.

1. Get your novel copyedited.

Yes, I want you to write the cleanest copy you can the first time. However, I can almost guarantee that there are plenty of typos in the manuscript. More than you could guess. And more importantly, more than you could notice.

Nature of the beast, folks. Noticing our own typos is no easy thing.

Which means you need someone else to copyedit it for you. And more than that, you'll need someone who won't copyedit the voice out of your story. Who can tell a mistake from an intentional deviation from the grammatical norm.

So you'll need someone who uses a light touch, not a heavy touch.

You can look for a pro, but if you do, remember you're looking for a *copyeditor*. Not *any other kind* of editor. Just a *copyeditor*.

If you have a detail-oriented friend, you might be able to get them to do it if you're willing to trade some services.

You probably don't want to have another writer do this, though. Many writers will want to rewrite your work and might not know how to stop themselves. This will make a lot more work for you than it will save.

Note: there are professional writers who are also professional copyeditors. You *should* be able to trust them not to rewrite your work. But check their references first.

If you don't have a detail-oriented friend, and you can't afford the rates of the pros, you might check out the local journalism schools. College students shouldn't cost as much as the pros, and if you find someone majoring in Journalism, they should do a pretty good job without getting into the ... critiquing issues you're likely to find in the English department.

2. Find a trusted reader.

I know I told you not to give your novel to your friends and ask for opinions. And I stand by that.

However.

A trusted first reader is worth their weight in gold.

What do I mean by a trusted first reader?

Well, I imagine that you have friends who like to read. I'm not talking about the writers, right now. Not unless those writers are well down the road from you (in which case they likely don't have time to do this for you).

I'm talking about *readers*. The ones who go through dozens of novels or more every year. They don't just like to read now and then. They read *a lot*.

Those people have a strong sense of what a novel is. And if they read in the genres you write, then you can trust that they also have a sense of whether or not your novel fits the genre you think it does.

Not always as obvious as you might think.

So. Take a friend who reads a lot and ask *them* to read your novel. And don't just blithely ask what they think, either. Give them, in advance, a list of questions you'd like them to answer when they're done.

I suggest these three, simple questions.

* Did the opening draw you in?

* Did the story hold you? If anything threw you out of the story, please note it.

* Did the ending satisfy you?

That's it. Those are the most important things that you need to know.

Now, that second question can lead you astray, if you let it. Because a well-meaning reader might think they know *why* something threw them.

But as Neil Gaiman has said, "When people tell you something's wrong or doesn't work for them, they are almost always right. When they tell you exactly what they think is wrong and how to fix it, they are almost always wrong."

Trust your own sense of story.

You might be tempted to add more specifics to those questions. Fight that urge. That's underconfidence talking.

Trust your inner storyteller.

3. Publish that beastie!

Now. *How* you publish this novel is up to you. I'm going to talk more about publishing in the next chapter.

But publish it.

You might be thinking, "But it's my first novel! It can't be any good!"

Trust your inner storyteller. Publish that novel.

You might be thinking, "*I've* read this thing and I think it sucks!"

So? Writers are always terrible judges of their own work.

Trust your inner storyteller. Publish that novel.

You might come up with all kinds of excuses to delay. To put off the risk of exposing your writing to the world. Of people not liking it.

You might try to talk yourself into waiting *one more novel* before you start publishing.

Trust your inner storyteller. Publish that novel.

Let me tell you a secret.

Back sometime before 2007 — and I don't mean *just* before, this was a while ago — I was still writing stories now and then. I only wrote them for myself. I never intended to show them to anyone.

I cringe, now, when I go back and look at any of those stories. To me, those are some of the worst bits of fiction ever committed to the page.

And yet those stories have made me hundreds and hundreds of dollars. They might have passed the thousand-dollar mark. I'd have to check.

The reason they've made me that money?

Because I didn't leave them sitting on my hard drive, gathering e-dust.

When I first became curious about indie publishing, I needed stories to test the waters with. So I grabbed those, because I knew I'd never want them associated with me anyway.

And I published them under a pseudonym. Just to learn what I was doing.

Readers don't care what I think of those stories. Readers don't care that I didn't know what I was doing when I wrote them.

But some readers buy those stories. Read them. And look for the others.

So trust your inner storyteller. Publish that novel. Under a pseudonym, if you like, but publish that novel.

Give the poor thing a chance to find an audience.

And while you're at it, show your inner storyteller that you believe in what you're doing.

Publish. That. Novel.

QUICK SUMMARY

Well, you either finished your novel or you didn't.

1. If you *didn't* finish

Why didn't you finish?

Was it word count?

If so, did you have a *compelling reason* not to finish, or an *excuse*? If the former, no problem. Writing will still be there when you recover from whatever curveball life threw at you.

If it's the latter, well, then you need to think about whether or not this gig is really for you. Because if you can't get to your desk and produce words on a steady basis, you're going to have a hell of a time trying to make it as a writer.

Did you hit a story snag you couldn't unravel?

If so, did you go back and look at my advice in Part Two of the warm-up? If you did, and you still had trouble, it's probably a confidence issue.

I suggest you go read and work through *Creating Short Fiction* by Damon Knight, then try going through this book again. Damon

Knight's book should help you develop confidence in your storytelling.

Did you just run out of time?

If you passed the deadline, and your story's still going, *finish it.*
Keep going to your desk every day and writing your 1,667 words every
day until the novel's finished.

Then, when you finish it, accept my congratulations and move on.

2. If you *did* finish

Congratulations! You have a completed novel that *you wrote.*
That's excellent. So, what should you do with it?

First, here are some things you *shouldn't* do:

Don't turn around and rewrite your novel.

Don't send your novel to an agent.

Don't post your novel to a website.

Don't throw it at all your friends and ask for opinions.

Don't give it to your critique group!

Okay. If you're not sure why you shouldn't do any of those, go
back and read the section again.

Now, here are some things you *should* do:

Get your novel copyedited.

Find a trusted reader.

Publish that beastie!

Oh, and one last thing. If you take no other advice from me, at
least take this:

**If you want to build a career, look get your advice from people
who are further down the road you want to travel.**

CHAPTER FIVE

WHAT'S NEXT?

LOOKING TO THE FUTURE

ALL RIGHT! NOW, IF YOU'VE GOTTEN TO THIS POINT IN THE BOOK, I'M pretty sure you've written a novel.

Might've been your first try at the thirty-day novel challenge. Might've been your sixth. Might've been something you did that was completely unrelated to any kind of challenge, but you came back to this book anyway, to see what I'd tell you next.

If it's any of those, congratulations! You stuck with it and wrote a novel!

(And if you haven't written a novel yet, but still want to, *hang in there*. You can do it!)

The question now is...

How do you feel about writing novels?

If you're done with it.

Maybe you feel complete with the whole experience, and don't feel the desire to do it again.

That's just fine. You've tried it. You've succeeded. That puts you light years ahead of the countless masses who talk about writing a book someday, but never even attempt it.

Also, congratulations on knowing yourself well enough to recognize that it's not for you. You're sparing yourself a lot of hassle. (Of course, you should still publish the book you wrote.)

If you want to write another one ... someday.

That's just fine too. Go do all the other things that are calling to you. Come back and write another novel when you feel like it.

Here's the thing, though, that I want to make sure you understand.

What you're talking about is writing as a hobby, not a career. And that's cool. Don't let anyone tell you it isn't.

But don't make the mistake of thinking that you're building a career as a writer, if you only ever get around to writing when the mood strikes you.

You're building a *hobby*, not a career. And again, that's fine.

But if you want develop a *career* in writing, you need to find the motivation to write on a steady basis.

If you can't wait to start the next one.

This, my friends, is a pretty good sign that you're serious about wanting to build a career as a writer. There are no guarantees, and it won't be easy, but if you can keep that fire burning, you can make it.

I'm pulling for you.

Now. While the hobbyists might gain some benefit from the rest of this chapter, it's really written with you folks in mind. So read through it, and take your next step into a bigger, wider world.

I can tell you. It's beautiful here.

KEEP LEARNING THE CRAFT

Hey! You wrote a novel! That's awesome!

Now you're ready to really start learning how to write.

What ... you think I'm kidding?

I assure you. I'm not.

You learned a fair amount, just in writing that novel. And that's good. But the truth is, learning the craft of writing is a never-ending process.

There's always more to learn.

Always.

And you should never be arrogant enough to think you're done. That you know everything you need to know.

You don't. Not today. Not next year. Not five years from now. Not ten years from now. Not twenty years from now.

Never.

Because there's *always more to learn*.

So, let's talk about how you can approach this. And personally, I recommend not using one or two of these methods, but *all* of them.

In fact, I'm not listing *all* the methods by which you could keep learning the craft. Not by a long stretch. But these will get you started.

1. Read fiction

Keep reading, folks. If you want to write more short stories, *read* short stories. Read magazines and anthologies and collections. If you want to write more novels, *read* novels. Read lots of them.

In my opinion, you should always have at least one book going.

Now. One of the common pop culture images of the writer — and for some reason people glom onto this as something romantic or desirable — portrays the writer as unable to enjoy novels / short stories / movies / whatever, because they can't stop seeing the flaws.

That isn't a good thing, folks. That is a problem. And if you're caught up in it, you need to learn to get past it.

Because if you can only see the flaws when you read, you're not reading like a writer. You're reading like an editor.

And no one is paying you to edit the novel you just bought.

You won't win any prizes if you find more mistakes than anyone else. What you *will* do is deprive yourself of the joy of reading.

And as a writer, you *need* to maintain the joy of reading.

Which means you need to start reading like a *reader* again. The way you read when you fell in love with reading in the first place.

So if you're at the point where you're only seeing the flaws in everything you read, try to relax.

Stop thinking about the *words*, and follow the *story*. If it helps, go back and reread some beloved novel from your youth. Something you know so well you could recite it from memory.

Read that novel. And then read something else you know well. Keep at it, until you're having fun reading again. Until you're getting caught up in the story, and not worrying about the words, or any mistakes or flaws.

Right now some of you are thinking, "But what if I don't like the book? Shouldn't I figure out why?"

No.

If you start reading a book and you don't like it, don't worry about *why* you don't like it. It's probably just a matter of taste. Put the book down and read another instead.

I know. Some people feel the need to finish reading every book they start, even if they hate it. I used to be like that.

Well, I hereby give you permission to abandon reading anything you aren't enjoying. Go find something else and read that instead.

But keep reading. And have fun with it.

Oh. Long as I'm talking about reading fiction...

Read broadly. Read outside your normal genres. Try reading all kinds of things. You may discover that you love something you never even considered.

ABOUT BESTSELLERS

So, there is this tendency, especially among writers early in their careers, to deride the bestsellers. To say that the likes of James Patterson or Stephen King or Dean Koontz or Clive Cussler or Jeffery Deaver or Danielle Steel or Norah Roberts or whoever can't write.

Don't make the mistake of buying into that crap.

Those people are some of the best storytellers around. That's *why* their books sell so well and so consistently. Some of them might not be to your taste, but I strongly suggest giving them a chance. You might learn something.

Speaking of which...

2. Learn from fiction

I'm calling this out separately. Because I want to get you *reading for fun* first. That's the most important thing.

But...

When you run across something cool. Some scene that really affects you, or some opening or ending that just blows you away, take note.

Don't do anything about it yet. *Finish enjoying the whole novel first.*

But once you're done, *then* go back and look at the bit you liked so much. Read it over again, slowly. Try typing it in, and see how it feels coming through your fingers.

Consciously you might still not figure out how or why it works. But you're telling the storytelling part of your mind that you liked that technique. And the storytelling part of your mind will learn from it.

Someday, you might even find yourself using that technique in a story. It's happened to me.

3. Read nonfiction

Whether your interests include history or castles or clothing or celebrity biographies or something else entirely, there are nonfiction books about things that interest you.

Keep reading them. In fact, read more of them. Find books on subjects you might not normally read, and read those too.

Yes. I want you doing *all kinds* of reading.

Now, I don't expect you to study nonfiction books, the way you might a novel.

But you can learn a lot from them. And what you learn from them may have a salutary effect on your writing.

You never know where the next inspiration will come from. You never know where you'll find the answer to a question you didn't know you had.

For example, I've gotten all kinds of ideas — as well as useful information — from a book about the life of Caterina Sforza. A book I never expected to find myself reading. Except that I was wandering through a bookstore one day, after watching a few episodes of *The Borgias*, recognized her name, and became curious.

So I don't know if reading nonfiction books on whatever topics *technically* counts as education about writing craft. But it can definitely improve your writing and your storytelling. So I say it counts.

4. Read books about the writing craft

This is probably what you expected me to talk about a moment ago.

Nope. I consider reading books about the craft of writing worth its own entry.

There are lots of these things out there for a reason. They all have something to teach. **And if you learn even *one* thing from any given book, reading it was a good use of your time.**

It might even just be that you run across an idea for the third or fourth time, but *this time* it sinks in. You never know.

One warning though.

Before you buy or read a book on the craft of writing, check the author's credentials.

If they're telling you how to write novels, *make sure they've written novels*. Not just one or two, either. Look for someone who's written a lot of novels.

If they're telling you how to write in a genre, check and make sure they've got the credits in that genre. Don't let someone teach you to write romance, if they've written a dozen thrillers and *one* romance novel. Or some other combination along those lines.

Is the book written by a "consultant" rather than an author?

Skip that book and move onto the next.

Learn to write from *writers*. Not from editors, agents, publishers, consultants, book doctors, gurus, or whatever.

Learn to write from writers.

If right now you're wondering about *my* credentials, good. If you didn't check them before, check them now. They're right here in this book. Go look at them. If you're reading this in paperback, they're in the front. If you're reading an ebook, they're in the back.

Go look. I'll wait. I don't have anything to hide here, because I *do* have the credentials.

And so should the author of any other book on writing.

5. Take classes on writing

Okay, first things first. Remember what I said above about checking credentials? That applies *double* here.

For some reason, lots of writers get a single novel published — or maybe even two! — and then start running around teaching classes about writing novels.

Forget that crap.

Find the pros out there who teach as a way to give back to their community. Learn from *them*. I'll list a few in the Resources chapter, but feel free to dig around and find more on your own. There are plenty.

Just check their credits *before* you sign up for their classes.

That'll save you a lot of time and money.

6. What about an MFA?

For those who don't know, MFA in this case refers to a Master of Fine Arts degree in Creative Writing. It is the most advanced degree in Creative Writing that can be achieved, academically.

Should you get one?

Honestly, that's a personal decision, and one I can't and shouldn't make for you. I will tell you that readers don't care one way or the other.

Do your research. See what you think of the programs, and whether or not you think they'll help you get where you want to go. Check out the credentials of the faculty. Do they have careers you want?

Personally, after I finished my NaNoWriMo back in 2007, I went on to get an MFA. But I also went to a program that was run entirely by writers, and where I could study under a writer who had won awards I'd love to win, myself.

That experience and education was great for me. But even so, I developed writing habits that I needed to later unlearn. Still, I'm glad I did it.

But your mileage may vary.

KEEP LEARNING BUSINESS

All right, folks. Here's a piece of news you may not want to hear.

But do not skip this chapter. Because you need to hear it.

If you want a career in writing, you need to start learning about business.

I know, I know.

But you're an *artiste!* A creative! You want to just write! Let the pencil pushers and the number crunchers handle the details.

If any of what I wrote in the preceding paragraph sounds like you — or even has you saying *yeah* — then stop whining.

Because this is the hard truth, folks.

If you want a career in writing, you need to learn business.

The moment you started writing books, you became a writer.

But the moment you started *selling* books, you became a businessperson.

And that means you need to learn business.

Pure and simple.

Yes. If you really wanted to, you could hire someone to handle all that nasty "business" stuff for you.

Two problems there.

One, you're *paying* someone to do it, which means outgoing

expenses that might outstrip your writing income. Especially in the early days.

Negative cash flow. Not good. It means you're setting yourself up to operate at a loss, right out of the gate.

Hardly a recipe for success.

Two, if *you* aren't the one keeping an eye on the money, you won't know if the person you hired is stealing from you.

I hate to be the one to break this to you, but some people in this world are dishonest. And some people, who might not otherwise be dishonest, find themselves *strongly* tempted by unchecked opportunities.

Just to name one example, I know of authors who discovered — the hard way — that their agents were pocketing translation rights payments. And simply not telling the author that those payments came in.

This happens.

If you dig around online, you can find all kinds of news stories about authors who were ripped off by people they trusted to handle their money.

You need to keep one eye on the money.

And you need to learn business.

Don't worry. I'll help you get started. I'll include some recommendations in the Resources chapter. Books and classes that are author-friendly, to help you begin learning business.

Because you're going to need to read books about business.

You're going to need to take classes about business.

Believe me. I know. I came to my career in writing with no idea how accounts receivable and accounts payable worked, what exactly cash flow was, what a business plan really was, how to budget for the coming quarter, and on and on.

I knew next to nothing about business.

I've been playing catch-up ever since. And while I've learned a lot, I'm still studying. Still learning more, all the time.

Because just like learning craft, learning business never stops.

Now.

I'm sure I've scared the hell out of some of you.

Sorry about that. But it was necessary. Because this is not something you can get around. This is not optional.

If you want to build a career as a writer, you need to learn business.

But that's all right. Really. Because as you develop your understanding of how businesses work — and thus how your writing business can work — you'll see opportunities.

You'll start seeing the good side of understanding the business end of things.

It can even be lots of fun, if you let it. I know I never thought I'd enjoy learning this stuff, but honestly. I really do.

Plus, it can give you *great* fodder for stories.

LEARN COPYRIGHT

I almost included this in the section about learning business. Because copyright is the basis of your business.

But honestly, this topic is so important that I wanted to call it out and give it its own section.

Folks, you *must* learn copyright.

Let me try to explain.

See, that novel you wrote? It's not just a book.

It's a set of t-shirts, based on characters and settings and quotations.

It's action figures.

It's a movie. *And* a television show. *And* a multi-voice audio production. *And* an audiobook.

It's a video game. *And* a boardgame or three. *And* a card game or four.

All those things and more — oh, so very, *very* many more — are all out there. Waiting to happen.

And all of them, based on that novel you wrote.

And there's more.

Those short stories you wrote? All those things I just listed, they're all true for those short stores too.

Every single one of those short stories.

The truth is, when you create a story — no matter its length — what you're creating is a gigantic ball of rights that you can license. For money. Some of those rights can be licensed more than once simultaneously. Others on a recurring basis.

Here. Imagine a ball of multicolored yarn. No two strands are exactly the same color or pattern.

And that ball of yarn is forty feet tall.

Every tiny strand of yarn in that giant ball? It's a different right that you can license from your *one* story.

Each and every strand of yarn is a potential source of income for you.

The options are almost limitless. They're up to your own imagination, and as a writer I know you have a great imagination.

So from any one story, you have many, many ways you can make money.

But here's the thing.

All those options?

All those income streams?

Right now they're closed to you. Functionally nonexistent, beyond the one or two most obvious strands.

But you can open up the way to every strand in that giant ball of yarn.

All you have to do is learn copyright.

Learn copyright, folks. Learn copyright, and begin to realize *just how very many ways each and every story you write can make you money.*

Copyright is how you make your money, folks.

Learn copyright.

The Copyright Handbook from Nolo Press.

Buy it. Read it. Keep it nearby. Read it again. Read it on the toilet. Read a page or two over breakfast.

Don't feel you have to try to read the whole thing at once. You don't. Not by a stretch. You can work your way through it at whatever pace you like.

But read it.

Read that book, and start realizing just how many strands of yarn go into that giant ball. Then smile, and know that every time you write a story, you're creating another giant ball of yarn, with just as many strands.

All that money. Just waiting for you to understand that it's out there waiting for you.

Publishing your novel in paperback and ebook? That's just the beginning. Two strands of yarn. Barely scratches the surface of all the things you can do.

Learn. Copyright.

PUBLISH!

Part of the pop culture image of the writer includes having a drawer or a trunk full of old manuscripts that "will never see the light of day."

Oh! The embarrassment of those early stories! No one must ever see them!

It's a load of crap, folks.

All right, look. I'm not saying you should dig up every little thing you've ever written and publish it proudly. No one needs to see every poem full of your horrible teenage angst, or whatever.

Of course, at the same time, I'm not saying that you must hide those things from the world. Maybe you're proud of those teenage angst poems. In which case, go for it! Put together a collection.

There may be people waiting to read them.

My point is this.

Somewhere in your life there's a dividing line. A point where you started taking writing seriously. Trying to tell stories the best way you can.

Maybe you crossed that line in your sixties. Maybe in your thirties. Or maybe you crossed it in high school.

Maybe you just crossed it, starting with the short stories you wrote during the warm-up for your thirty-day novel challenge.

When you crossed that line doesn't matter.

But everything you've written since then is something you poured yourself into.

That effort should be rewarded. And the result should be published.

Tell your inner storyteller that you value the time you spend writing. Publish what you write.

Look. If you're reading this, the chances are good that you hope to develop a career in writing. And if you want to develop a career in writing, you need to publish what you write.

Not some of it.

Not most of it.

All of it.

Publish every single story. Under a pseudonym, if you like. If you aren't sure you want a given story associated with you — because of its genre, topic, or whatever — using a pseudonym is fine.

But publish it all.

Because you never know what will take off. What will be the thing that readers respond to.

Folks, writers are terrible judges of our own work. We don't even always know what *genre* we've just written.

And no matter what some people try to tell you, no one knows in advance what will be a hit and what won't.

So publish everything. Give your stories a chance.

All right. Here endeth the lesson. You either believe me or you don't.

Let's move on to what your options are for publishing.

First, for the short stories.

1. Writers of the Future

If you don't have much in the way of publishing credits right now, you really ought to consider submitting short stories to the

Writers of the Future contest. You can enter quarterly. The prize money is really good. And if they publish your story, they pay well too.

Oh, and their contracts tend to be good.

2. Professional Magazines and Anthologies

If you go to a website like Duotrope or Ralan or the Submission Grinder, you can find a list of magazines and anthologies that pay professional rates to license and publish short stories. Check them out.

Double-check their contracts, though. Some of them send you "new writer" contracts the first time, which are ... not good. But you can always negotiate better terms, and you should.

3. Semipro Magazines and Anthologies

These are magazines and anthologies that *pay*, but don't pay *professional rates*. Personally, I suggest starting with the professional places, but if they've all rejected your stories — see the section on Dealing with Rejection — you might consider trying a couple of semipro markets.

Personally, I suggest setting a minimum rate you'll accept — perhaps five cents a word, or three cents a word — and not taking less. Value your writing.

In fact, don't feel the need to settle for less than professional rates, if you don't want to. I'm just letting you know this is an option.

Oh, and definitely double-check those contracts. Some of these guys cobble theirs together from other people's contracts, and the results can be scary.

If you want to find these, again, I suggest using a website like Duotrope or Ralan or the Submission Grinder.

4. Nonpaying Markets

Just what they sound like. Websites and magazines and anthologies that want to publish your stories and not pay you a dime.

Yeah, forget those guys.

Value your writing, folks.

5. Indie Publishing

You can always indie publish individual short stories. Or assemble them into a collection. Or both. You can do all kinds of things with your short stories. I'll talk a *little* more about indie publishing down below.

A note about Submission Fees

Some magazines want you to pay them to read your story. They call this a "submission fee." Some claim that this "enables" them to pay their writers, or whatever.

Okay. This is up to you. But me, I won't even consider sending those guys a story. I don't *pay people* to read what I write.

And as for "enabling" these places to pay writers, *they* aren't paying their writers. *Other writers* are paying their writers.

I think that's messed up. I don't want anything to do with it.

Now. Onto the novels.

1. Big Publishers

Once upon a time, there were hundreds of reasonably big publishers that a writer could send manuscripts to. So many that they could be made to bid against each other for your book.

Ah, those halcyon days.

They are *so* dead.

The big publishers kept buying each other. And then getting bought out by huge international conglomerates.

As I write this, there are something like four or five big publishers left.

And yeah, yeah, I know. The pop-culture image of the writer

involves getting one of these publishers to pay millions and millions of dollars for one book, and yadda yadda yadda.

Yeah.

Look.

Forget these guys.

Consider this:

* Nobody ever asks if a publisher should have a day job.

* Nobody ever asks if an editor should have a day job.

* Nobody ever asks if an agent should have a day job.

Now go look around online at *all* the discussions about not only *whether or not* a writer should have a day job, but *how long they should expect to keep that day job.*

The publishing industry involves billions of dollars a year.

And yet, writers — you know, the ones who *create* everything that gets sold by publishers — are somehow the only ones expected to have secondary sources of income?

Doesn't make sense, does it?

You know why that is?

Well, let me tell you.

Remember what I said about learning copyright? Well, these big publishers want to buy that whole damned ball of yarn, and they only want to pay you a pittance for it.

And then *they* get to make as much money as they want from it. And *you* get that pittance they gave you. *Maybe* to include some royalties. It's been known to happen.

I'm not kidding. Their contracts are atrocious. If you go to these guys, they *might* give you a few thousand dollars. But you'll lose *tons* of earning potential. And you're not likely to ever get that earning potential back.

My advice — forget them. Don't even bother trying with these guys.

Some of you are going to ignore that advice, though.

So if you're going to go to these guys anyway, please, do yourself two favors.

First, learn copyright. So that you *understand* what you're giving up when you sign that contract.

Second, hire an attorney — an *intellectual property* attorney who specializes in literary work — to go over your contract and ensure you understand what you're signing.

That second thing? That's going to be expensive. But not nearly as expensive as signing a bad contract.

2. Small and Medium Publishers

Sadly, most of what I said about the big publishers applies here too. They may be smaller, but they tend to follow the lead of the bigger publishers. Which does not make them author friendly.

And their contracts aren't necessarily any better.

Heck, one medium press wanted me to *guarantee* that readers could "follow the instructions" in my book safely.

I'm talking about a novel. An *urban fantasy* novel, full of magic, monsters and more. Heck, at one point a character makes a deal with a *sidhe*. And no way in this or any other world am I going to advise *anyone* to deal with the Fae, let alone *guarantee* that it can be done "safely."

The clause was a holdover from their days as a nonfiction press. But they refused to remove it. And, wonder of wonders, I refused to sign.

Now, I've heard tales of some of the medium presses that are actually fairly author friendly. So maybe they exist. If you want to go this route, do your research first.

Also: learn copyright. And hire an IP attorney to help you with your contract.

Remember. *A bad deal is worse than no deal.* You're better off walking away than signing a bad contract.

3. Indie Publishing

All right. As you might have guessed by now, this is the direction I think you should go. Indie publishing allows you to control the rights to your work — that whole, beautiful ball of yarn — while affording you the opportunity to make as much money as you can.

Through indie publishing you can get your books into all the world's bookstores. And libraries. And you have the options to come up with all sorts of other ways to make money with your stories.

Omnibus editions. Limited edition hardbacks. Kickstarters. Patreons. Subscriptions. The options are almost endless.

Yes, this will take time. Yes, this will likely cost some money. But we're talking about small, up front costs. And when those costs are paid, the profits are all yours.

There's a learning curve to it, of course. It involves other skills than just writing.

Just consider that part of learning business. Because now you're learning the business of publishing, and starting your own publishing company. Which is pretty darned cool.

Heck, if you like it, you can get to the point where you start publishing other authors as well. That's up to you.

I suppose, right now, some of you are expecting me to tell you how to get started with indie publishing.

Sorry.

That's *way* outside the scope of this little book.

Besides, by the time you read this, the best practices may have changed. Which means that what I'd tell you wouldn't do you much good.

Some of the resources I'll give you at the end of the book will help. But really, the best thing you can do is dedicate some time every day to researching indie publishing online.

And don't be afraid to experiment. One of the advantages of indie publishing is that it's quick and easy to make changes. Both if you make a mistake, and if you come up with something you like better.

Also, I do have to point out, you don't have to do it all yourself. Goodness knows I don't. It's a question of whether you want to spend time or money. Bringing in other people saves you time but costs you money.

Of course, depending on what skills those people bring, the money you pay them may pay you serious dividends. Book covers can be like this.

All right. I'll stop there. Do your research. Learn to publish.

It's worth it.

DEALING WITH REJECTION

I hate to say this, but rejection is just another part of life for writers.

If you want to send your short stories out to magazines and anthologies, some of them will get rejected. Heck, possibly *all* of them will get rejected for a while.

For example, there's a professional editor who has rejected every story I've sent him. And I've sent him ... oh, it must be more than forty stories over the last few years.

Sometimes he doesn't like the opening. Sometimes he doesn't like the ending. Sometimes he likes both the opening and ending, but something about the story didn't "sell" him.

Does that mean those stories aren't good?

Well, if you believe that, explain this:

Several of those stories have sold to other professional magazines and anthologies. Just as they were.

Here's another example.

Remember that story I mentioned earlier? The one I watched get rejected by five editors on a panel, before the sixth and final editor said she loved it?

Those were five professional editors who didn't like my story.

Several of whom had bought others stories from me, either before or since or both. And yet, this story fell short for all of them.

Who cares? The sixth one was the only one who matters. *Because she bought it.*

Here's the thing about rejection.

It's true that at a certain stage of a writer's career, the craft isn't there yet, and their stories will get rejected because the writer isn't good enough yet.

But after a certain stage of development, it's not story quality anymore.

And as the writer, *you* won't know when you've crossed that line. So don't worry about it. Just keep learning your craft and writing your stories, and sending out those stories to magazines and anthologies.

So, wait a second.

If it isn't *quality* that's getting your story rejected, what is the reason?

Most of the time, it's taste.

Editors aren't hired because they know "good" stories from "bad" stories. They're hired because someone believes that their taste will appeal to the audience of that magazine or anthology.

That's it, folks.

Taste.

Well, all right. There are other reasons too.

Sometimes a story gets rejected because the editor just bought another story that was too similar. Or because the theme of the story doesn't fit in with the other stories that editor already bought.

And there are other reasons.

Sometimes the time of day the editor reads a story makes a difference. If your story was near the bottom of today's pile, your story might not get as much attention as a story from the start of the day.

Now, some editors know that mood, time of day, and so forth affect them. And they'll give a story a second chance the next day.

But that depends. If they're looking at a pile of hundreds of manuscripts, they may not have time for that second look.

So what point am I trying to drive home?

Rejection isn't always about quality.

Have confidence in your writing. If a story gets rejected by one editor, send it somewhere else.

My first professional sale was bought by the eighth market I sent it to. I've had others bought by the sixth, or the ninth.

All of those are professional sales, paying professional rates.

So when rejections come, what should you do?

1. Shrug it off.

Don't take it personally. It isn't personal. Heck, that editor who's rejected some forty or more of my stories? He and I have a long-running conversation going. And I'm pretty sure that every time he reads one of my stories he hopes it's the one he can finally buy.

I hope so too.

2. Send that story back out.

Just because one editor doesn't want to buy a story doesn't mean that another editor won't love it. Keep that story out there, looking for a home.

Oh. One more thing.

3. Don't rewrite that story!

Some editors will suggest changes. Well, unless they're offering to buy your story if you make those changes, ignore them.

Trust your storyteller. You told your story your way. Have faith in that.

All right. If they reject the story pointing out some glaring story error — *but Mary can't be the one who solves the crime, she died on page seven!* — or if they complain about the sheer number of obvious typos or something similar, then maybe you should take a look at their comments.

For example, sure. Maybe Mary *did* die on page seven. But maybe there was a compelling reason she was the one who could solve the crime at the end. You should probably take a look at the manuscript and make sure that reason comes through clearly.

Sometimes the story in your head doesn't always make it to the page right. That's part of learning the craft.

But otherwise, forget their suggestions. Trust your inner story-teller and get that story back out there.

And don't worry about rejection. It's just part of being a writer. Take is as a badge of honor, if you like.

Some writers like to celebrate their rejections.

I don't do that. My goal isn't getting rejections, so I don't think they're worth celebrating. I just don't think they're worth stressing over, either.

Far as I'm concerned, I don't give a rejection any more time or attention than noting the market that rejected a story so I don't send them the same story again.

And then, I move on. And I suggest you consider the same approach.

STAY HEALTHY

Okay, folks. If you want to have a long-term career as a writer, you need to maintain your health.

Maybe this sounds obvious to you. If so, terrific. But I'm going to cover it anyway. Just to make sure.

1. Eat Right.

Lean meats. Vegetables. Fruits. You know the kinds of things you should be eating, and if you don't, consult a doctor.

Or, heck, I'm sure there are hundreds of free articles out there, written by doctors, that'll cover the basics for you.

The point is, writing is a career that can lead to excessive snacking, quick runs for fast food, and all kinds of bad habits.

Fight those urges. Eat right.

Your body — and that includes your brain — responds to the kind of fuel you give it.

All right. You get the point.

2. Exercise.

Exercise isn't just good for the body, folks. It's good for the mind. So whether you like to walk, run, cycle, play a sport, go hiking, or whatever, get some exercise. Preferably on a regular basis.

I can tell you from personal experience that there's a good side effect to getting regular exercise, too.

Ever since I started running at lunchtime three days a week, it's helped my writing. While I run on the treadmill — listening to music — my mind wanders. Inevitably about the book I'm writing.

I get the coolest ideas while I'm running. And I'm getting them in the middle of my writing day. So when I get back to my desk, my fingers are flying as soon as I sit down.

And that feels *awesome*.

3. Sleep.

I know, I know. Some of you, right now, can only find writing time by getting up a little early or going to bed a little late.

I understand. I do. I've done it myself.

Nevertheless, make sure you get as much sleep as you *can*. Goodness knows, here in the United States, sleep deprivation is a common thing. And it's not good for us.

Don't short yourself on your sleep any more than you have to. And look for opportunities to get a little more.

Everyone's personal requirements are a little different. Personally, I'm happiest if I'm getting at least seven hours a night. I know others who can't function without eight.

Figure out where you fall on that spectrum.

Do what you can to make sure you get what constitutes "enough" for you.

And if you can stretch that a little sometimes, by sleeping in, it's a good idea.

Oh. I'm not big on napping myself, but some writers swear by it, for solving story problems. Sounds worth a shot to me.

4. Get regular check-ups.

Get your annual physical. See your dentist twice a year. Get your eyes checked. And your hearing.

This way, if something *does* go wrong with your health, you catch it sooner rather than later.

5. Stretch.

During your writing day, if you write at a keyboard, get up. Walk around. Stretch your arms and wrists. Try not to spend more than twenty or thirty minutes at your keyboard without getting up for a minute or two.

You don't have to stop thinking about your story. But your body will thank you, over time, for those little breaks.

6. Finally, if you *do* have a chronic health problem...

All right. I'm not qualified to address this, but I wanted to bring it up, because it might affect some of you. If so, you should first consult your doctor. I am not a health professional, and I do not pretend otherwise.

However, I do know a writer who has managed to have a very long, successful career, despite chronic health issues. And she's written a book about it. *Writing with Chronic Illness* by Kristine Kathryn Rusch. She can tell you a lot more about this than I ever could.

PATIENCE

Building a career in pretty much any field takes time.

Writing is no different.

Sure. There's a *chance* that your first book will become an international sensation and catapult you to fame and fortune.

Well, fortune, anyway.

Fame is something that happens to other people. If you're hoping for fame, you're better off going for a different career. Even the most famous writers you can name draw less attention from the media and the public than minor film and television actors.

Personally, I find that comforting.

Anyway. Fortune, that can happen. It can even happen overnight. It can even happen with your first novel.

But it's not the way to bet. Because, frankly, the odds are about the same as winning the lottery.

And you definitely shouldn't *expect* instant success. Not with your first novel. Not with your tenth.

Folks, settle in for the long haul.

Learn to take your joy from writing and publishing. From the process of telling stories. From completing each story, each novel. From putting that story or novel out there, for others to buy and read.

You will build your audience.

You will build your income.

But these things will take *time*.

And the truth is, there's no easy way to say how long these things will take.

Now, there are some people out there who will tell you that if you follow their methods, you'll make X amount of money within your first year or whatever.

Yeah. Most of those people are *selling* their method. Think about that.

Forget those guys.

Forget the quick schemes. Forget about trying to play algorithm games over at Amazon, or any of that crap.

Have patience.

Keep learning. Keep writing. Keep publishing.

Build your audience one reader at a time. One story at a time.

Let the rest attend to itself.

That, folks, is how you build a career.

KEEP WRITING

All right. I've left the most important one for last.

Congratulations! You've written a novel!

Now get back to your desk and do it again.

And again.

Keep at it, folks. Keep writing. Short stories, novelettes, novellas, novels. Essays. Poems. Whatever it takes to keep you writing.

Keep telling stories.

Because that's what it's all about.

You need to keep getting to your writing desk on a steady basis, and telling stories.

Because that's what it takes to build a career as a novelist.

Some people will tell you to take time off between novels. To "reset your mind" or something like that.

That's crap. Get back to your desk.

Look at it this way.

Take a moment and imagine your novel winning some major award. Maybe the Hugo, if you write science fiction or fantasy, or the Edgar if you write mystery. Whatever.

Imagine the awards ceremony. Some famous writer is the presenter. Maybe your favorite writer. And they're calling your name because you won! Imagine going up to the front. Accepting the award. Maybe making the speech.

Now imagine something else.

Imagine that your novel has set fire to all the sales charts, and it's bringing in millions and millions of dollars. Can you imagine that? Seeing your novel atop all those lists? Seeing the numbers of your bank accounts go through the roof?

Guess what.

Those were two completely unrelated stories. And your mind just handled both of them, without any break in between.

So get back to your writing desk and tell another story.

Everything else depends on your doing this.

Every day, folks. Back to the desk. Hitting your word count. Starting new stories, finishing those stories, then getting those stories out for publication.

Then getting back to your desk and doing it again. And again. And again.

Because this is what a writing career is all about.

Have fun with it. I sure do.

QUICK SUMMARY

Once more, remember. The summaries are not a replacement for the sections themselves. Just reminders to help you keep in mind the major points.

If you only read the summaries, you're cheating yourself. And you know what I think of that.

Anyway. On with the summary.

So, what do you think? Is writing novels what you want to do for a living?

If not, cool. Now you know. Good for you, for giving it a shot.

If it is, this is what you need to do.

1. Keep Learning the Craft.

This is a never-ending process, so learn to enjoy it.

2. Keep Learning Business.

Writing a story makes you a writer. Selling a story makes you a businessperson. So now you need to learn business. Don't leave it to others, because that's a good way to get ripped off.

3. Learn Copyright!

Can't stress this one enough. Every story you write creates a giant bundle of rights — remember the yarn ball analogy — and each of those rights is a potential income stream for you.

But only if you understand copyright.

Learn copyright.

Do it.

4. Publish!

Get those stories out there in the world, making you money. Preferably via indie publishing, but if you really must try going to one of the big publishers, remember. Learn copyright, so you know what you're giving away for next to nothing. And hire an IP attorney, so they can explain exactly how bad the contract is.

5. Dealing with Rejection.

Rejection is part of a writer's life. Don't take it personally, because there's nothing personal about it.

6. Stay Healthy.

You'll get a lot more written if you stay healthy, folks. Eat right. Exercise. Sleep. Get regular check-ups. Take breaks during your writing day and stretch.

7. Patience.

Don't expect huge sales with your first novel. Building any career takes time, and writing is no different. Have patience and keep at it. Build your audience and your income one reader at a time, one story at a time.

8. Keep Writing.

This is what it's all about, folks. Get back to that writing desk day after day, and tell more and more stories. Everything else depends on this. Have fun.

CHAPTER SIX

IN CONCLUSION

ONE MORE THING

Now, throughout this book I've made references to *Telepathy 1A*, the novel I wrote during NaNoWriMo 2007.

And yet, those of you who looked over my credits might have noticed that *Telepathy 1A* is not listed among my novels.

Hey! That's right! What gives, Mr. Publish Everything?

Well, folks, the truth is, I made a lot of the mistakes that I've warned you about. I sent that novel off to agents. I made changes to it based on feedback that I really should've ignored.

Oh, the list of mistakes I made with that poor novel.

Well, I ended up leaving it on my hard drive, collecting e-dust, for a several years while I went off and studied the craft. I was convinced that it was a "first novel" and the sort of thing that belonged in a trunk for the rest of its life.

As I said. I made *all kinds* of mistakes that I hope to help you avoid.

In the end, though, I did start doing things right, where that novel was concerned.

I picked it up again a few years later. Around the time that I was finishing my MFA. And I remembered how much fun I had just sitting down every day and letting the novel unfold through my fingertips. How I'd loved the characters and their story.

In other words, I remembered the fun.

That was the first thing I did right.

The second started when I looked at it again. I could see that it wasn't the novel I'd written anymore. I'd polished away what I'd loved.

So I didn't try to "fix" it. And that's important.

Instead, with the characters and the story in my head once more, I set aside *Telepathy 1A* and started writing the whole novel over, from page one, word one.

I did no copying and pasting. I never referred back to *Telepathy 1A*. I just started writing the novel over. Redrafting it from scratch.

It came out differently, in a lot of ways. It even started in a different place.

That makes perfect sense, because I was a different person and a different writer when I wrote that novel the second time.

Did it come out better than my original version of *Telepathy 1A*?

We'll never know. That first version is gone.

The new version of that novel is called *Surviving Telepathy*, and it wound up kicking off a trilogy.

So please. For the sake of your novel. Pay attention to my advice. Don't make the same mistakes I did.

Trust your inner storyteller.

FINAL THOUGHTS

And so we come to the end.

I hope this has been useful for you, and that I've been some help to you on your path toward a career in writing.

If I could leave you with any one thought, it would be this:

Have fun.

I know. That seems so simple it's almost facile. But it's *important*.

Folks, once you start making money with your writing, it can be easy to start putting *pressure* on your writing. To start worrying about whether or not a given story idea will sell. Or worse, thinking about the things that are selling right now, and trying to steer your own writing that direction.

Don't do it.

That way lies madness.

When it comes time to write, forget about the rest of the world.

Tell the stories that you *burn* to tell. Tell the stories you want to read and can't find anywhere else. Tell stories that frighten you. Tell stories that make you laugh and cry.

Write *fiercely*.

Write the stories you can't *wait* to write. The ones the make you rush to the keyboard in the morning, and that you find yourself thinking about before bed.

That's what I mean by "have fun."

Within you are stories only you can tell. And somewhere out there are readers, yearning to read those stories.

So tell *your* stories.

And have fun.

RESOURCES

A Starter List

Here are just a few books and classes you might benefit from. There are many, many more. More categories, too. I don't even mention podcasts, for example.

But this should help get you started.

1. Books

Craft first.
Crafting Short Fiction by Damon Knight
I learned a lot from this book, and I think it's worth reading.
On Being a Dictator by Kevin J. Anderson
All about how to write by dictation. And he should know. He's been doing it for decades.
Writing into the Dark by Dean Wesley Smith
A great book about letting go of outlines, or worries about where the story is going, and trusting your inner storyteller.
Writing with Chronic Illness by Kristine Kathryn Rusch

Kris has been doing it for a long time, so if anyone can help you figure out how to do it, she can.

And now, a few business books.

The Copyright Handbook, published by Nolo Press.

Buy it. Read it. Reread it. Keep it at your writing desk. I can tell you mine's in arm's reach right now.

Cash Flow for Creators: How to Transform Your Art into a Career by Michael W. Lucas

If you're new to learning business, this book can be a great help.

The Writer's Business Plan by Tonya D. Price, MBA

A very detailed book, and it taught me a lot I didn't know about business plans.

Business for Breakfast series published by Knotted Road Press.

A very good series of books to take you from a beginning pro to an advanced pro. Well worth checking out.

The Million Dollar Writing series published by WordFire Press

A good collection of books written by long-time pros, on a variety of topics.

2. Classes

WMG Workshops (https://www.wmgworkshops.com/)

There are both online and in-person classes (though not so in-person during the pandemic, of course), covering both craft and the business of writing.

They're taught by either Kristine Kathryn Rusch or Dean Wesley Smith or both.

I've taken a number of classes from them, and I highly recommend them. You can learn a lot from these two. Not only are they great writers, they're *terrific* teachers.

Dave Farland's classes. (https://mystorydoctor.com/)

I've taken some of Dave's lectures through his website, and found them quite good. He's another one who's not just a long-term, successful writer, but also an excellent teacher.

He also has live and online workshops, but I haven't tried those yet myself.

Superstars Writing Seminars (https://superstarswriting.com/)

I've attended Superstars only once, but I had a great time and learned a good deal. It's not the quality that keeps me from coming back. It's scheduling conflicts.

SIGN UP FOR STEFON'S NEWSLETTER

Stefon loves to keep in touch with his readers, and loves to keep you reading. The best way for him to do both is for you to sign up for his newsletter.

Sign up at http://www.stefonmears.com/join

If you sign up for Stefon's newsletter, you get...

- Monthly updates about his publishing and travel schedules
- His latest news, in brief, and answers to reader questions
- A free short story for signing up
- List-only offers and occasional specials
- Plus a free short story every month!

ABOUT THE AUTHOR

Stefon Mears has more than thirty books to his credit, and he never stops writing. He earned his M.F.A. in Creative Writing from N.I.L.A., and his B.A. in Religious Studies (double emphasis in Ritual and Mythology) from U.C. Berkeley. He's a lifelong gamer and fantasy fan. Stefon lives in Portland, Oregon, with his wife and three cats.

Look for Stefon online:
www.stefonmears.com
himself@stefonmears.com

www.ingramcontent.com/pod-product-compliance
Lightning Source LLC
Chambersburg PA
CBHW031124020426
42333CB00012B/224